MAR 2015

Robbery

First published in 2012

A catalogue record for this book is available from the British Library

ISBN: 978-0-857331-74-8

Published by Haynes Publishing, Sparkford, Yeovil,
Somerset BA22 7JJ, UK
Tel: 01963 442030 Fax: 01963 440001
Int. tel: +44 1963 442030 Int. fax: +44 1963 440001
E-mail: sales@haynes.co.uk
Website: www.haynes.co.uk

Haynes North America Inc., 861 Lawrence Drive, Newbury Park, California 91320, USA

Images © Mirrorpix

Creative Director: Kevin Gardner
Designed for Haynes by BrainWave

Printed and bound in the US

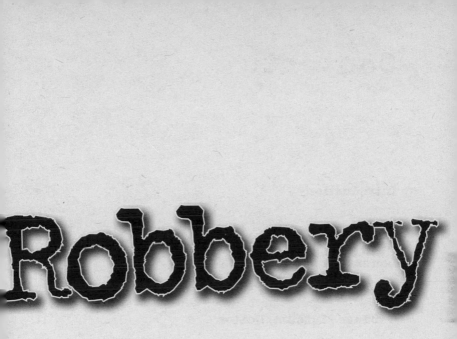

Robbery

From The Case Files of

THE **PEOPLE** and **M**_{DAILY}**irror**

Claire Welch

Contents

Frauds and Swindles

Introduction

Theft, unfortunately, is something that many people experience at some point in their lives, whether it's the loss of a mobile phone, money, a handbag, a suitcase on a train, or property taken from their home or place of work. Having an experience of this sort often leaves the victim feeling upset and angry, stressed and vulnerable. Something belonging to them has been taken, and victims can feel violated as a result. Robbery can be more serious for the victim in that it involves taking something of value by force, or threat of force, depriving an individual of their property – or their company's property – through fear and intimidation. The victim is led to believe that they may be subjected to violence at any point during the robbery. There is real fear for the victim: robbery is a violent crime. Muggings, looting, carjacking, extortion, piracy and many other forms of crime, including armed robbery and aggravated robbery – involving the use of a deadly weapon – all come under the banner of robbery, which is a statutory offence in England and Wales.

The Great Train Robbery of 1963 saw an innocent train driver hit over the head and badly injured when £2.6 million was stolen from the Glasgow–London mail train. Some 20 years later, six armed men, posing as security guards, gained entry to the Brinks Mat high-security vault at Heathrow Airport. After dousing a guard with petrol and threatening to set him alight, they made off with £26 million in gold bullion and diamonds. And, in May 1990, bonds worth £292 million were robbed from a professional in the financial industry who was held up at knifepoint. The police believed that the man responsible for the crime was the small-time crook Patrick Thomas from south London, who was found shot dead before he could be charged.

Robbery does not have to include a huge level of force and the fear does not have to be great in order for this type of crime to qualify as a robbery by use of force or fear. Robberies can, and do, occur almost anywhere at any time. All this form of crime needs is someone motivated to take what is not rightfully theirs from another person, in either a public or a private place and with enough time in order to do it. Most robberies are committed by one person against another (who may, or may not, be known to one another) in less than one minute – and many victims are not harmed unless they resist the perpetrator. However, other robberies are carried out by gangs whose members are carefully hand-picked and who know exactly what they're doing, how they're going to commit the crime and get away with it, and how to dispose of their takings without themselves (or the loot) ever being traced. But there are also those who will give the police the vital tip-off that they need in order to catch some, if not all, of the perpetrators. Nevertheless, in the technological age of the 21st century, the police and the wider authorities are really up against the criminals who are organized, sophisticated and dangerous.

Robberies, and those who commit them, are nothing new. Piracy and the pirates who commit violent acts at sea have been around since commercial trade routes opened up across the world's oceans. Highwaymen travelled by horse to carry out their robberies while footpads robbed on foot. These robberies, which often targeted vulnerable stagecoaches and unsuspecting travellers, took place from the Elizabethan era right up to the early part of the 19th century. Many pirates and highwaymen faced the gallows if caught. As policing in and around London became more organized at the start of the 19th century, and banknotes (more easily traceable) began to replace gold coins, the highwaymen all but disappeared on Britain's heaths and commons.

Looting (also known as sacking or pillaging) often took place as a result of war, rioting or natural disaster (and still does today). One of the first documented cases of looting took place in 455 in Rome, when the Vandals invaded successfully and sacked the city following the death of Valentinian III. During the Second World War, both Germany and Japan engaged in the systematic looting of valuables, which proved catastrophic for the countries they looted; the overall total was worth tens of billions of US dollars. In 1977, mass rioting and looting took place in New York following the New York Blackout. In more recent times, the Haiti earthquake in 2010 saw looting, blamed on the slow distribution of relief aid. And, in 2011, the London riots led to chaotic looting around other areas of Britain – in Manchester, Liverpool and Birmingham as well as in other smaller towns and cities.

In another part of the world, much earlier in the history of violent crime, during the mid-1880s, train robberies in America's old west were particularly commonplace. Payroll shipments were a major target, despite being protected by highly committed "expressmen" who willingly risked their lives in order to safeguard the money. As time progressed, robbers used dynamite to gain access to the safes on board. These criminals would either board the train and wait for an opportune moment in which to strike, or they would derail the train in order to rob it, taking cash and other valuables from the passengers at the same time.

Art theft was, and still is, big business. Robberies of valuable artworks have been carried out with the intention to either sell the art or to use it for ransom. Many artworks are never recovered. This is still true today, where only a handful of stolen artworks are ever returned to their rightful owners. High-profile art galleries and museums have installed sophisticated, high-spec security. However, there are still poor security measures in some areas, which inevitably lead to the loss of multi-million-pound pieces while providing potentially huge returns for the criminals. There are often not enough gallery or museum attendants on duty – although these types of crimes are not often subject to "smash and grabs"; security cameras can be blocked and paintings could often benefit from more secure fastenings or locks. It is often presumed that when an art robbery takes place there is likely to be an "insider" helping with information or making access easier for the criminals.

Stealing from banks with firearms is another violent crime. Most often committed in cities and large towns, bank robberies are usually reported extremely quickly, and while the criminals might have plenty of escape routes in more urban areas, the emergency services can respond rapidly and in greater numbers. Unlike other forms of violent crimes, bank robberies are often committed during daylight (when banks are open), have multiple witnesses and the criminals are often caught on CCTV. In the UK, banks that are robbed are statistically likely to be robbed again within a three-month period.

Another particular lure for the violent criminal is the potential for large amounts of money within today's metals market. Scrap metal prices tend to rise on a worldwide scale – and copper, aluminium, lead, brass and bronze can all fetch lucrative profits in the right climate. These materials are sold for their value as raw materials, which can be scrapped, recycled and used for producing new products. Metal thefts have been on the increase since 2006 – particularly in the UK, where it has become one of the fastest-growing crimes in recent history. The estimated cost to industry from robberies involving metal products is more than £380 million. It is, of course, extremely difficult to identify stolen metals, unless the object involved is recognizable (for example, a bronze statue). Today, church roofs and schools are common targets for thieves, as are statues, ornamental features, plaques and even manhole covers. Metal is serious business, and while some police forces have been slow to treat these crimes as serious, others are clamping down on violent criminals who are defacing and defiling the British countryside, and stealing from religious buildings and legitimate metal companies.

Rhinoceros horn has also become hot property in recent years. While poaching has long been the bane of the authorities where wild rhinos are concerned, thieves are now targeting museums and robbing their prized exhibits of their iconic features. It's no surprise, really, with real rhino horn fetching somewhere in the region of £60,000 per kilogram in the Far East, where it is prized for its alleged medicinal qualities.

Statistically most robberies are committed by young men under the age of 25 who, more often than not, have some connection to drugs. Firearms are the most likely weapon of choice, while "strong-arm" tactics such as threatening behaviour, punching, kicking and other forms of fighting come a close second. Knives or other stabbing or cutting implements actually make up a small percentage (around 9 per cent) in terms of favoured weapons. Most violent crimes – other than bank robberies – are committed under the cover of darkness (with more crimes carried out during winter months). Experts believe that, in the majority of cases, criminals are not intending to use their weapons on their victims. However, victims of crime do not always behave in the way that the perpetrator expects – and many criminals will use their threatening tactics or weapons if they have to. This might be as a result of a "cool head" and a calm need to force the issue or make an escape, but equally the criminal might be panicked into taking drastic action.

But it's not just the use of force that has been prevalent in robberies carried out over the last century. We have witnessed trusted employees swindling their firms out of millions, and respected doctors defrauding their patients of their family's inheritance. Whatever the intended target, criminals need to meticulously plan all aspects of their robbery if they are to evade capture and enjoy the spoils of their labours, as police forces around the world take action to return the property to its rightful owners.

Robbery

Art Heists

Louvre

Mona Lisa (1911)

Argentine con man Eduardo de Valfierno allegedly set up six interested buyers of Leonardo da Vinci's painting *La Gioconda*, more commonly known as the *Mona Lisa*, before persuading Louvre employee Vincenzo Peruggia to steal it from right under the nose of his Parisian employer. French art restorer and forger Yves Chaudron was commissioned by Valfierno to forge six replicas of the masterpiece, which were then shipped to various parts of the globe before the heist took place. Posing as a marquis, Valfierno persuaded six influential buyers that they were all going to receive the original. Following the robbery on 21st August 1911, all six forgeries were delivered to their intended buyers, who all believed that the marquis had stolen the painting for them personally. Valfierno's contact with Peruggia (who cut the painting out of its frame with a sharp knife or razor and hid it under his coat before walking calmly out of the Louvre) was limited and, after the robbery, the two men did not meet again. But, is this story true or false?

The painting was only noticed missing on 22nd August 1911 shortly after noon. A telegram was sent immediately to the minister for fine arts – who, like many French officials, was away on holiday for the month of August – informing him that the painting had been stolen.

Would-be visitors to the museum were told that a water pipe had burst and that the Louvre was closed (it was shut for a week). Thus an investigation got under way. At first, staff and officials believed that the painting had simply been removed from the frame so that it could be photographed for marketing purposes – and a thorough search of the museum took place. However, when no trace of the *Mona Lisa* was found, it was reluctantly agreed that Da Vinci's 16th-century masterpiece had been stolen.

Although recognized today as one of the world's most famous paintings, the *Mona Lisa* wasn't appreciated on an international scale until the mid-19th century, when the emerging Symbolist movement began to associate the enigmatic painting with their ideals about feminine mystique. Leonardo da Vinci began the painting in 1503 at his home in Florence, Italy. It was his habit to leave a painting unfinished for some time, often many years, before returning his focus to it once again and it is believed that the *Mona Lisa* was no exception. He is thought to have returned to the painting (oil on poplar panel) following his move to France in 1516, when he was invited by King François I to work at the Château du Clos Lucé, and to have completed it just prior to his death in 1519. After Da Vinci died, the king bought the painting, which was eventually given to Louis XIV and moved to the Palace of Versailles. It was then moved to the Musée du Louvre following the French Revolution (1789–99). The painting had a short spell on the bedroom wall of Napoleon at Tuileries Palace before being returned to the Louvre.

Despite many attempts to identify the sitter and many suggestions from various authorities and art historians, the authentication of Lisa came only in 2005 at the University of Heidelberg, when an expert discovered a 1503 note in a margin of an original document. The painting is a portrait of a seated woman, Lisa del Giocondo, wife of the wealthy Florentine silk merchant Francesco del Giocondo, and was commissioned by the family to celebrate both the birth of their second son and their new home. The world has discussed the qualities of the painting over many centuries – not least because it is believed that Da Vinci kept a true likeness of the subject (her lack of obvious beauty for one thing) and the ambiguous smile on the lips of the virtuous woman.

At the time the painting went missing, there was no known value as to its worth, but one thing was for sure: the masterpiece was priceless. Estimates were proffered at around £100,000 and experts were convinced that a buyer would be willing to pay far more. Known as "the picture of the beautiful smile", Leonardo's biographer, Vasari (whose book was published in 1550), wrote how the artist had kept musicians, singers and jesters all around his subject so that she would be entertained in order to "dispel the melancholy which is so easily imparted to painted portraits".

The Mona Lisa had been on display in the same positioning in the Salon Carré for five years when it was stolen in 1911. Four iron pegs on which the painting had been hung were found by the painter Louis Béroud instead of the masterpiece. The investigation gave the authorities nothing to go on and no clues were found. The painting – so simply hidden under a coat and removed from the museum – was seemingly lost for ever. But, two years later, the painting was discovered in Florence and the news announced in the press by Professor Credaro, the minister of public instruction, in Rome on 13th December 1913. Peruggia was under arrest and the painting back in the possession of the authorities. The Italian patriot had grown tired of waiting to dispose of the original and had attempted to sell it to the Uffizi Gallery in Florence, where his deception was uncovered. Peruggia claimed that the dark eyes and appealing manner of the painting had brought out his patriotism and that this is what had inspired him to "abduct" the work. He confessed to cutting the picture from the frame and ensuring that it arrived in its country of origin.

Before being sent back to Paris, the painting was displayed throughout Italy. Peruggia was sent to an "asylum" for six months, and the story was told in considerable detail in a book written in 1913 by M Cassellari, entitled *Chapters in French Crime*. The *Mona Lisa* has survived for more than 500 years since it was breathtakingly created by Leonardo da Vinci, despite some severe acid damage caused by a vandal in the mid-1950s and a rock being thrown at it (among other attacks), once it was protected behind bullet-proof glass.

But the question is: did Peruggia work for Valfierno? It's not really clear, although the two men did meet fleetingly at the Louvre on one occasion. Peruggia claimed he never knew Valfierno, who sent copies of the *Mona Lisa* all over the world long before the actual heist and then waited to send them out once the painting was stolen. It's known that all Valfierno needed was for the *Mona Lisa* to disappear so that his fakes could be sold undetected. But was this really all part of a well-thought-out plan with Peruggia at the core? The question remains unanswered.

Russborough House

(1974, 1986, 2001 and 2002)

In June 1973, a millionaire's daughter helped police with their inquiry into a £100,000 art theft from the home of Lieutenant-Colonel James Dugdale near Axminster in Devon. Dugdale and his wife had been away from home at Derby Day in Epsom when the robbery occurred, but police were able to recover most of the stolen property from the couple's own daughter. In court, Dr Bridget Rose Dugdale, 32, cross-examined her own father on the second day of her trial at Exeter Crown Court, telling him: "I love you, and if your life were in danger I would wish to stand between you and that danger." But, she went on to add: "At the same time, I hate everything you stand for." The doctor of philosophy chose to defend herself in court, and asked her father to tell the court how much money he had given her. It transpired that Colonel Dugdale had given his daughter – known as Rose – £82,000 when she broke her connection with the family trust in 1972. She claimed that the money had been used for the Tottenham Civil Rights Centre and to help the poor. She and her lover, Walter Heaton, 43, a Tottenham civil rights worker and an ex-convict, both denied robbing her parents' country home or dishonestly handling stolen goods.

Rose Dugdale and her parents had battled over her future for some years. While academic high-achiever Rose wanted to carry on with her education, her parents longed for her to become a lady. She was sent to finishing school – which she loathed – and a debutante season was arranged in London following her expensive education. Rose only agreed to the season when her parents compromised and brought in a tutor to give her a crash course so that she could apply for university. The endless rounds of cocktail parties, dinners and balls probably did more than anything else in Rose's life to turn her against the trappings of affluence and wealth. Rose was accepted at Oxford, where the rift with her parents grew wider. Following Oxford, Rose lectured at London University and worked for various United Nations agencies. Her work in Tottenham then took off and it was there that she met Walter (Wally) Heaton.

Rose was found guilty of robbing her parents' home in Devon on 22nd October 1973. Heaton – also found guilty of handling £82,000 worth of paintings, silver and gems – was sentenced to six years for his part in the robbery. Following the guilty verdict, Rose launched into a long tirade against the judge, Mr Justice Park, who told her that she would be remanded while he ordered medical reports to be taken. She was to be sentenced following the outcome of the reports. Rose had repeatedly told the court that she had been threatened by a gang and ordered to take part in the robbery of her parents' home. Her sentence was eventually decided – two years' imprisonment; however, it was suspended for two years and Dugdale walked free from court at the end of October 1973. In his summing up, the judge said: "For an individual of her intellectual gifts and training, a custodial sentence would only further reinforce bitterness and resentment, but the challenge of practising what she preaches might prove a turning point." He went on: "I think the risk of you ever again committing burglary or any other offence of dishonesty is extremely remote."

Yet, less than four months later, in February 1974, Dr Rose Dugdale was back in the press when she was believed to have gone into hiding in Ireland. Police were looking for the former Oxford graduate, after searching homes in England and Ulster, so that they could charge her under the Explosives and Firearms Act with conspiring to smuggle arms and explosives to Ulster and illegally possessing guns and explosives.

Early in 1974, 12 paintings – worth more than £8 million – were stolen from Sir Alfred and Lady Clementine Beit who were assaulted when their home, Russborough House, was robbed of some of its masterpieces. Situated two miles south of Blessington in County Wicklow, Russborough House was bought by Sir Alfred in 1952 specifically so that he could house his impressive art collection there. The house, designed by architect Richard Cassells (who firmly believed in the Palladian style of architecture in 18th-century Ireland), was built by Joseph Leeson in 1741 and was the perfect location for Sir Alfred's collection. The first robbery at Russborough had Irish Republican Army (IRA) involvement, organized by Rose Dugdale to raise money and to obtain the release of Heaton from jail. Dugdale, by now a self-styled revolutionary, was brought before Dublin's Special Criminal Court on 6th May 1974 charged in connection with the world's biggest art robbery. She had been "hiding out" with a man at a seaside cottage in County Cork, but had been discovered quite by chance when a quick-witted policeman who called at the house in the course of his enquiries thought that Dugdale was suspicious. The couple had given their name to the landlord of the property as Merrimee (along with a home address – Levaston Street in London – which did not exist). When Sergeant Patrick O'Leary called at the cottage in Glendore, he felt something was wrong and returned later with a party of officers in order to raid the premises. Police found a hand grenade, along with the three most valuable paintings that had been stolen from Russborough House, including a Goya and a Vermeer, while the other paintings were found in the boot of a car outside the house. The man renting the cottage along with Dugdale was long gone, but the police believed that they were hunting for IRA boss David O'Connell. Rose Dugdale was given nine years for her part in the robbery but was again in court in November 1974 when she was found guilty alongside two men of hijacking a helicopter for an IRA bombing raid on an Ulster police station. She was also wanted for questioning by police in England for arms smuggling.

Russborough House came under attack again in 1986 – some eight years after it formally opened to the public – when thieves escaped with paintings valued at more than £30 million on 21st May. Described as the world's biggest art raid, police were called to the house of diamond millionaire Sir Alfred after an alarm went off. They could find nothing wrong and left the premises but, hours later, a security check uncovered the theft of 18 paintings including masters by such luminaries as Goya, Gainsborough and Velasquez. The haul also included the last privately owned Vermeer painting in the world, which by itself was worth an estimated £30 million on the open market. Police did not want to rule out Provisional IRA involvement and confirmed that the heist was the work of experts. It was believed that blackmail was the motive behind the robbery. Later, on the same day as the robbery, seven of the less-valuable paintings were found in a van parked near Russborough House.

It was 1988 before anything further was heard of the remainder of the stolen paintings, when some were offered for sale in Holland. An informer provided the Dutch police with photographs of 10 masterpieces, including works by Vermeer, Goya, Gainsborough and Rubens. The informer, believed to have been appointed by members of the art underworld as a middleman, offered information to Dutch detectives in return for immunity from prosecution. At this time, police believed that a Dublin criminal gang was responsible for organizing the robbery and this was later confirmed with the ringleader identified as Martin Cahill – known as "The General". Paintings from the 1986 robbery were found in England, Ireland, Holland and Turkey. In 1993, Goya's *Portrait of Doña Antonia Zárate* was also recovered.

In 2001 and 2002, Russborough House was again the target for art thieves, who managed to get away with far fewer and less valuable paintings than had been achieved in the first two robberies. Most of these were returned to the collection following police investigations into a gang, led by Martin Foley, an old associate of Cahill's. Vermeer's *Lady Writing a Letter with her Maid* and Gainsborough's *Madame Bacelli* were both stolen during the two thefts in the early 2000s, but subsequently recovered by the Garda. Then, in August 2002, after a lengthy surveillance operation in Dublin, police retrieved Ruben's 17th-century *Head of a Man*. Stolen 16 years previously by crime lord Cahill and his 13-strong team, the £20 million masterpiece was found by the Garda's arts-and-antiques squad, who were hopeful that more of the paintings would then be discovered. The painting was found in perfect condition and immediately returned to Sir Alfred's collection at Russborough. The motive behind Cahill's robbery of the valuable paintings was believed to be funding his plan to become the main drug boss in the UK. Cahill had been selling weapons to both the IRA and their arch-enemy, the Ulster Volunteer Force (UVF). He was gunned down by an IRA hit man in 1994. Four of the stolen paintings that were returned had actually been on the walls of Russborough House since they had been painted for the property in the 1750s. All four, by the French artist Claude-Joseph Vernet, had been an important part of the house and its estate for more than 260 years.

Today, the most valuable of the Russborough (Beit) Collection are held more securely in the "Beit" wing of the National Gallery of Ireland, while others are still housed in their original setting.

Gardner Museum, Boston

(1990)

American art collector, patron and philanthropist Isabella Stewart Gardner (1840–1924) began her extensive art collection when she inherited a large sum of money from her father in 1891. It began her vision of a collection that should be made available to the public. Gardner's first major acquisition came in 1892 when she bought Vermeer's *The Concert* at auction in Paris. When her husband, John L Gardner, died in 1898, she was able to realize their dream of building a museum in which the growing art collection could be housed.

Buying land and choosing a site in the Fenway area of Boston, Massachusetts, Gardner commissioned the architect Willard T Sears to build her a museum modelled on the palaces of Venice from the Renaissance period, in which she remained completely involved in every aspect of the design. When the museum was complete, Gardner was extremely careful about the layout of the artworks within the building, ensuring that each and every piece and collectable was properly positioned so that the immediate benefits could be seen from the outset. She cleverly mixed works from different areas of art – combining sections where textiles mixed with paintings, and furniture nestled comfortably with sculptures and other artworks. Gardner had the help of the eminent art historian Bernard Berenson (1865–1959), who had helped her collect more than 70 pieces, including a Botticelli.

On 1st January 1903, the museum opened its doors to the public for the first time in a lavish grand opening attended by Boston's influential set. Gardner was keen on all aspects of art and the art world and often invited artists, scholars and performers to experience the museum and its works for themselves. This legacy is still in existence today with extensive programmes of concerts, education, displays and an artist-in-residence scheme. The collection itself is extensive and consists of photographs and letters (from ancient Rome, Europe during the Medieval period, the Renaissance, 19th-century France and America) along with paintings, furniture, textiles, sculptures, architecture, silver, ceramics, manuscripts, drawings and rare books. Paintings that Gardner painstakingly collected include works by Matisse, Whistler, Botticelli, Raphael, Michelangelo, Rembrandt (*Self-Portrait*), Titian (*The Rape of Europa*), Degas and Sargent (*El Jaleo*). There are also letters written by T S Eliot, Oliver Wendell Holmes and Sarah Bernhardt, and Dante manuscripts.

Gardner stipulated that the museum should be available to all. While an entrance fee is charged, the museum's doors lie open for free to anyone named Isabella. For nearly 100 years, the museum was a sanctuary for priceless works of art to be savoured and enjoyed by the masses. Then, on 18th March 1990, two Boston police officers calmly walked into the museum and began helping themselves to some of the 2,500 artefacts and artworks on display. These two robbers – obviously disguised as police officers – told the security guard that they were responding to a call. As it was only the early hours of the morning, the guard on duty – in a break with protocol – let the two robbers through the security door. The two men then told the security guard that there was a warrant out for his arrest and asked him to step away from his desk. In doing so, he was steered away from the one and only alarm button and, as requested by the robbers, he summoned the only other guard on duty back to the main desk. The two guards were then handcuffed and taken to the museum's basement, where their hands, feet and heads were covered in duct-tape, and they were fastened to pipes to hold them securely. Knowing they would be safe until later in the morning, the two bogus police officers then concentrated their efforts on the museum's galleries, helping themselves to 13 works of art.

The morning security guard arrived to find that his colleagues were missing and the museum had been robbed. He immediately alerted the museum's director, Anne Hawley, and the Boston police. Vermeer's *The Concert* (one of only 34 masterpieces attributed to the artist and Isabella Gardner's first major purchase) was missing, as were five drawings by Degas and three paintings by Rembrandt (including his only known seacape). Also stolen was an ancient Chinese Ku, two other artefacts and a painting by Manet. Despite the fact that the investigation into the robbery remains open, no clues have been forthcoming and none of the stolen artefacts or paintings have been returned to the museum. There is a reward of up to US$5 million to anyone who can help investigators trace the perpetrators and the missing artworks, should they be returned safely and undamaged. The Gardner Museum, building on the legacy of its original creator, will undergo a huge expansion programme in 2012, which will double its size in a renovation estimated to cost $118 million.

Tate/Frankfurt

(1994)

Situated in the heart of the old city of Frankfurt in Germany, next door to the cathedral, is a thriving exhibition building known as the Schirn Kunsthalle, designed by Bangert, Jansen, Scholz & Schultes. Famous for the temporary art exhibitions it houses in 2,000 square metres, the Schirn Kunsthalle opened in 1986 following regeneration of the inner-city area after it was destroyed in 1944 during the Second World War. Exhibitions enjoyed eight years of uninterrupted serenity until disaster struck in 1994.

On 28th July that year, thieves lay in wait within the exhibition hall for the doors to close at the end of the day. They hid until night-time in order to steal three paintings, two of which were the works of Turner (*Light and Colour* and *Shade and Darkness*, on loan from the Tate Gallery in London) and one by Friedrich (*Nebelschwaden*, on loan from Hamburg's Kunsthalle). Those responsible were quickly apprehended after the robbery, in which a guard was overpowered. An art dealer and two thieves were eventually sentenced in 1999 to up to 11 years' imprisonment. However, the whereabouts of the paintings were still not known. The three convicted felons refused to divulge what had happened to the masterpieces and also would not give up the identity of those behind the heist. Insurance companies had little choice but to pay out to the two galleries involved: the Tate received £24 million for the loss of the works of art.

Police suspected that a man known as Stevo – a leading figure in the Yugoslavian (Balkan) Mafia – was responsible and that he tried to sell the paintings to another underworld contact based in Marbella, Spain. The two men could not agree on a price and undercover police from Germany then became involved in negotiations a year after the robbery. Stevo eventually agreed a price with his underworld contact, but when he asked for the advance payment to be double what was originally agreed, the deal broke down once again. Stevo was then arrested, but his lawyer, the renowned Mafia defence attorney Edgar Liebrucks, persuaded the authorities that there was insufficient evidence to prosecute the Yugoslav. The German authorities and prosecutors had seemingly little choice but to give up in their pursuit of the perpetrators.

Meanwhile, the Tate was determined to retrieve its two masterpieces if at all possible and, in 1998, paid an insurance company £8 million in return for ownership of the paintings, should they ever be found. Although the Tate had an insurance payout up to the value of £24 million (£12 million for each painting), having received the insurance money it meant that if the paintings were ever recovered then they would belong to the insurers. The Tate took a huge gamble when it paid out the £8 million in order to secure ownership of the masterpieces should they ever reappear.

Approval for the plan had been given by the gallery's supervisory board to its director, Sir Nicholas Serota, in a covert operation known as "Cobalt". Working undercover, two detectives from New Scotland Yard contacted Liebrucks, who negotiated on behalf of the Tate in a sensitive deal with Stevo. Liebrucks was effectively working for both sides in what would be an extremely delicate operation. Trying to retrieve something from the Balkan Mafia was not going to be easy. The Yugoslav once again doubled his advance price – however, Liebrucks had contingency plans in place to cover such an eventuality, and the deal for *Shade and Darkness* was complete.

The painting cost the Tate £1.7 million (the same price was also agreed for the second painting), plus costs of £100,000 to Liebrucks. Turner's *Shade and Darkness* was returned to its rightful home in July 2000 when it was transported back to London. The Tate paid Liebrucks compensation for his part in the deal, but things reached a stalemate when Stevo appeared to have lost interest in securing the second deal.

The deal for the first stolen painting had brought about an extremely unusual turn of events when the original owner paid for the return of their painting from those who were hiding it for the Balkan Mafia who had originally stolen it. Undeterred, the Tate kept faith that they would also recover their second painting and, in the autumn of 2002, Liebrucks was contacted by two men claiming that they had possession of the two other missing paintings. These men, Josef Stohl – who had hidden the paintings behind spare car parts – and his accomplice Hartmut Klatt, decided that they would play a dangerous game and sell the paintings behind the back of the Balkan Mafia.

It seemed likely that the two men had been given the paintings by Stevo for safe-keeping, and were willing to trade and sell them. The Tate bought back Turner's *Light and Colour* – and the two German men involved took a long holiday on the other side of the world. The painting returned to London just before Christmas 2002. Like the first painting brought back to the UK, it was confirmed as the original, and in good condition although without its original frame. On recovery of both the Tate's paintings, the Kunsthalle Hamburg then followed suit and employed Liebrucks for the purpose of retrieving their own masterpiece. The two Turners – two of the artist's most significant works – went back on show in London on 8th January 2003.

Although the paintings were welcomed back to the UK, there remained the question as to whether the Tate had pulled off an enormous coup by retrieving its own artworks, or whether it had, in fact, set the precedent for ransom in the robbery of valuable masterpieces. The Tate claimed that they had only ever paid for valuable information leading to the whereabouts of the paintings in order that they could be retrieved. However, there are those who believe that the money that was actually handed over to Stohl and Klatt was money paid for the actual paintings; it was described by some as ransom. However, it could be argued that the Tate acted in the best interests of the masterpieces; they belong to the public and the Tate believes they should be seen by the public. The paintings have now been back on display for more than 10 years, available to be admired and enjoyed by all.

Burglaries and Robberies

Houndsditch Murders

(1910)

Houndsditch, a street in the City of London, was first referred to by its name in the 13th century, due to the quantity of rubbish and dead dogs thrown into the ditch. The street marks the route of an old ditch running outside a part of London Wall, first constructed by the Romans. It was eventually filled in and forgotten until the Danes reopened the ditch in order to control access to the City. The street was a bustling thoroughfare connecting Bishopsgate in the northwest of the City to Algate in the southeast, which was to become the backdrop to the horrific murders of three City of London policemen on 16th December 1910.

Louisa Bentley was just days off her 34th birthday. She was celebrating her ninth wedding anniversary to Sergeant Robert Bentley, who was on duty in the City, and she was looking forward to the imminent arrival of their second child. Meanwhile, a group of revolutionaries from Russia were attempting to break into the back of a jeweller's shop on 119 Houndsditch, but they were heard by another shopkeeper who immediately alerted the police to the break-in. Nine unarmed officers descended on the property and two of the three sergeants present entered the house. Once inside, the policemen were confronted by a man standing in the near darkness at the top of the stairs. The two sergeants tried to speak to the man, but another robber entered the building through a doorway from the yard and both men began shooting at the officers. Sergeant Robert Bentley collapsed where he stood just inside the doorway. Sergeant Bryant staggered outside, while constable Woodhams ran to Bentley's aid. He was also shot by one of the gang members who was firing from inside the building. Sergeant Tucker was also shot by the gang and died almost instantly. The gang, knowing they were cornered, attempted to leave the building through the back entrance and Constable Choate managed to apprehend the robbers' leader, George Gardstein. The constable was injured by Gardstein's gun before being shot five more times by other members of the gang. However, the robbers also shot and badly wounded Gardstein, who they then dragged to Grove Street, more than three-quarters of a mile away (he died the following day.) Later, on the same day as the attack, Sergeant Bentley and Constable Choate also died as a result of their injuries. It was left to Louisa Bentley to tell the young couple's daughter, Kathleen, that her father had died. Louisa gave birth to their son just a few days later on Wednesday, 21st December 1910.

All three policemen were buried with the highest honours at Ilford Cemetery after a service held at St Paul's Cathedral in London. It was the first time that such a service was held at St Paul's for civil police and the occasion was marked by the presence of many dignitaries, including Winston Churchill and a representative of the king, groom-in-waiting Mr E W Wallington. A vast congregation crowded into the cathedral, including City and Metropolitan police forces, the fire brigade, the Salvage Corps, the lord mayor and the lady mayoress. At noon, the three coffins were met at the west door by the dean, Canon Scott Holland, the Bishop of Kensington, Archdeacon Sinclair and other clergy. Each coffin had a significant number of wreaths, including those sent by the home secretary and Mrs Churchill.

Following the service, a sombre procession of the coffins slowly made its way through crowded streets towards Ilford Cemetery, headed by the City Police band and a body of mounted policemen. The coffins entered the cemetery to the sound of Chopin's *Funeral March* and the *Funeral March* by Beethoven, before the burial service took place, conducted by the Bishop of Barking, Revd J S, Dean of St Michael's, Southwark. The following day, the press announced that police weapons – traditionally contained within police stations only to be used in emergencies – were out of date and trials were to take place to establish which weapons would best suit police purposes when dealing with modern-day robbers and criminals armed with efficient up-to-date firearms.

Just six days after the attempted robbery, two women were brought before the Guildhall Police Court charged with being accessories to the murders. Sarah Rosa Trassjonsky (also known as Rose Selinsky) and Luba Milstein – both described in court as skirt-finishers – were remanded until 29th December 1910. A day later, police announced that they had arrested a man, known as Yourka, whom they believed was involved in the murders. The information leading to Yourka's arrest had come from a young lad in London's West End, after a description of the man police were seeking had been released to the public. Police also had another man in detention, having been led by the youth to a house in Fairclough Street where associates of Yourka were found. In an attempt to gain more information leading to the arrest of other men in connection with the murders, police offered a £500 reward. The men they were looking for included a man named Fritz, formerly of Grove Street, who was a locksmith from Russia; Peter, known as "Peter the Painter" (also of 59 Grove Street and believed to be Russian); and a 26-year-old man (name unknown) who had a scar from a gunshot on his upper arm.

Detective Inspector Macnamara of Scotland Yard had visited a house in Turner Street, off Commercial Road (and just a few yards from Grove Street) on 22nd December, where he found photographs of those believed to be Russian revolutionaries. Letters addressed to the man known to be "Peter the Painter" were also found, although four different names were on the envelopes. Revolutionary literature and a card belonging to the Lettish Social Democratic Party were also found, while the landlady of the property confirmed that one of her lodgers wore a grey mackintosh (police had already established that Peter wore a coat fitting this description). The landlady stated that the man had moved into her house about three weeks before and had told her that he was a tailor's presser. She said he was visited on several occasions by well-dressed men, and added that one night, the previous week, he had definitely been out all night. She was unable to confirm the exact night. Dr Bernstein, carrying out the post-mortem on Gardstein, confirmed that the man was an inhabitant of the Russian Baltic province of Livonia.

On 26th December 1910, Osef Federof, 30, Jacob Peters, 24, and Zurka Dubof (Yourka), 24, were charged at the Guildhall Police Court with the murders of the three policemen, Sergeants Bentley and Tucker, and Constable Choate. A large crowd waited outside the Guildhall while the three men were questioned in court. A witness named Isaac Levi had come forward to give evidence that he had seen two men – whom he identified as Peters and Dubof – supporting Gardstein through the streets shortly before midnight on the night of the murders. They had pointed a gun at Levi and instructed him not to follow them. Levi also confirmed that there was a woman with the three men when he spotted them in the City.

The men were also charged with breaking in to 119 Houndsditch on the night in question. Peters, believed to be a cousin of Fritz and Dubof, was described as carrying away Gardstein, while Federof confirmed that he had been at the house in Grove Street that night, but had played no part in the break-in or murders. Isaac Levi, when questioned in court, stated that he had heard the gunshots coming from the Exchange Buildings as he made his way home from Liverpool Street. He had rushed towards the sound of the gunfire when he came face to face with Peters and Dubof. Along with the two women already in police custody, the men were detained on remand.

On 28th December 1910, the press revealed that further

developments had taken place in the police search over the Houndsditch murders. It was established that the man known as Gardstein was in reality a Russian named Poloski Morountzev, who had been lodging in a house in Gold Street, Stepney, since the early part of the year. At the house, police discovered several hundred loose cartridges, a belt containing Mauser soft-nosed bullets, a dagger and an automatic pistol of the same type used in the murders. Detectives also found a quantity of anarchic literature and works pertaining to the manufacture of explosives, together with a number of bottles containing nitric acid, nitro-glycerine and other ingredients. On 29th December, at the second day of the trial against the three men and two women, the discovery of the chemicals was discussed. However, there was no evidence to suggest that bombs had actually been manufactured by the group, as no explosives were found at the house in Gold Street. Mr and Mrs Kempler, whose house the Russian had lodged in, were in absolute shock when they realized with whom they had been sharing their home. A female witness described to the court how she had often heard strange noises coming from the Kempler's back yard at night, including knocking and scraping. The woman described how she and her family were often kept awake by someone who sounded as if they were chopping wood (for about an hour or so), which was followed by brushing or scraping until about 5.00am each morning. Meanwhile, it was announced that an inmate at Parkhurst Prison – said to have been acquainted with the suspects – was helping police with their inquiries. And, a cylinder of gas, weighing more than 55lbs and known to have belonged to the men in the dock, was found at

9 Houndsditch on the day of the murders. It had been moved there on a costermonger's barrow from its original location in Islington. Police were still desperately trying to find witnesses who could help them with details about the transportation of the cylinder, which was wrapped in brown paper and possibly taken in a box to the Exchange Buildings.

On 30th December, the five accused were brought together for the first time since their arrests, and put before Sir W Treloar who remanded the prisoners both for the murders (the two women charged as accessories) and the attempted burglary of a jewellery shop owned by a Mr Harris, who reportedly kept around £30,000 worth of stock in the shop's safe. The gang were suspected of using three houses in Exchange Buildings as a base for the attempted robbery. However, detailed charges were not given out at this point, as only formal evidence was heard. It was decided that any full opening statement would only be given once the police had had the chance to complete their investigations.

On 3rd January 1911, an informant told the police that two men – suspected of being involved in the Houndsditch murders – were hiding out at a house in Sidney Street, Mile End, in east London (where the dramatic sequel to the events that took place are since known as the Siege of Sidney Street). It was believed that Jacob Peters and Fritz – having been released on remand – were hiding in the house, and police descended on the scene to begin a pitched battle during which several were wounded. The home secretary, Winston Churchill, watched proceedings from a vantage point around the corner from the scene and called in the Scots Guards to help the police capture the two men.

For eight hours, police armed with shotguns and revolvers battled against the two suspects who fired on their would-be captors from an upstairs window at the property. The house eventually caught fire and the fire brigade were ordered to stay back, with the authorities believing that the men inside would lay down their weapons and leave the house voluntarily in order to save their own lives. However, the door to the property never opened and when firemen eventually entered the building to quench the flames, they found the two "wanted" men dead inside.

During the course of fighting, three police officers, a guardsman and five civilians were wounded by shots fired by the assassins, while five firefighters were injured in the debris after entering the burning building. It was one of the most extraordinary sieges that London had witnessed. At about 1.00pm, a puff of smoke had appeared from a second floor window of the house making it apparent to all concerned that the house was on fire. After an hour of flames, in which the fire spread to the ground floor, the fire crew that had been ordered to maintain the fire so it didn't spread to adjoining properties were slowly moved up the street. The front door of the property was kicked in and two badly burned bodies were found towards the back of the house at ground level. The siege was over: the hunted men had preferred death rather than capture. One of the men had been shot by police; the other had put a revolver in his mouth and taken his own life. Three people – two men and a woman named Bessie Gershon (an occupant of the sieged house who was not at home at the time of the battle) – were detained by police as they furthered their investigation.

Mystery after mystery seemed to dog the police investigation. They were fairly sure that one of the dead men was Fritz, but not sure that the other assailant was Jacob Peters. However, by the end of the first week of January 1911, they changed their minds and, based on witness statements in relation to the two men who were firing at the police, were convinced that "Peter the Painter" was indeed the second man at the house in Sidney Street. The inquest into the deaths of the two men was held on 5th January, which was attended by Luba Milstein, known to have been living with Fritz Svarrs at the house in Grove Street. Also attending, seated between two prison wardens, was Rose Selinsky who had nursed George Gardstein as he lay dying after the Houndsditch murders. Later that day, two other men – taken by police out of the house in Sidney Street before the siege began – were released, although Mrs Gershon was detained. It then transpired that "Peter the Painter" was not the second man to die in the fire and that the burned remains were that of a man known as Jacobs. The inquest heard how the two men were not shot dead as previously thought, but had been overcome by smoke and had burned to death.

Jacob Peters, or "Peter the Painter" continued to be a mystery for the police. No one seemed to know his real name or anything much about his history, although the police were confident that he was still hiding out in London. As a result of so much gunfighting and the deaths of five men, the police were issued with weapons for carrying out any organized raid that might bring the Russian to justice. Mrs Gershon was finally released by the police on 6th January 1911, once it was established that she had no involvement with the assassins.

The investigation into the death of the three police officers and the siege in Sidney Street continued throughout January 1911. Many witnesses came forward, giving the police vital information and clues; while the involvement of the home secretary in the events surrounding 3rd January were called into question. The chemicals found at Gardstein's lodgings and the gas cylinder removed from Islington continued to be investigated, and questions about whether or not the gang had been preparing a bomb factory were high on the agenda.

Meanwhile, Sidney Street became the scene of large crowds of sightseers; and Bessie Gershon gave a dramatic story of events on the night before 3rd January, stating that she had been threatened by the two men if she failed to keep quiet about their presence in the house. She had been called away from the house prior to the siege by her neighbour, Mrs Fleischmann, who had called to ask Bessie for help with her ill husband. Ten days later, the hearing at the Guildhall for Federof, Peters, Dubof (Yourka), Milstein and Trassjonsky (Selinsky) was resumed, with the case for the Crown against the five opened in full on 23rd January 1911. The hearing was adjourned a day later.

By early March, there were seven prisoners accused of the Houndsditch murders. However, William Treloar decided there was not enough evidence to convict either Sara Rosa Trassjonsky or new suspect Karl Hoffman. Both were discharged. Peters, Dubof and Nina Vassilleva (a cigarette-maker and new suspect) were thought to have enough evidence against them to charge them with being accessories after the fact of the murder of Sergeant Tucker by Gardstein (despite the fact that the revolver used was probably the property of Peters and had been dumped with Gardstein prior to the police finding him). Treloar also believed there was enough evidence against Vassilleva, Federof, Peters, Dubof and John Rosen (a hairdresser from Hackney, east London) for conspiracy to commit a robbery at the shop at 119 Houndsditch. But Federof was discharged on 15th March 1911. That same month, Sir Vezey Strong presented King's Police Medals to Louisa Bentley, and members of the Tucker and Choate families.

Robert "Bobby" Bentley, who was born just a few days after his father's death, died in Stockwell hospital at the age of three following a bout of diphtheria. Of the accused, none were brought to justice – with charges dropped, convictions quashed and acquittals given before convictions could be made.

Croydon Aerodrome

(1935)

On Wednesday, 6th March 1935, after spending hours amid the ceaseless bustle of the aerodrome, Scotland Yard officers brought to a conclusion their investigation into a robbery of £21,400 worth of gold from an Air Ministry safe at Croydon Aerodrome. Police knew that the raid had been executed by a gang of brilliant crooks who, using a private car, had a ready market for their loot in the UK. In spite of intense police activity at the aerodrome, under the direction of Superintendent Helby, the authorities could discover no clues at Croydon to assist them in their search for the raiders. The stolen goods were made up in three consignments of three bars of gold, each weighing 450oz and worth around £10,000. Also missing were around 800 English sovereigns, worth around £1,400 and American gold dollars worth around a further £10,000.

The gold had arrived at the aerodrome by road on Tuesday, 5th March in readiness for export to Paris and Brussels on Wednesday morning. But when a loader went to the strongroom where the gold had been deposited for the night, the driver discovered the door unlocked and the boxes missing. Less than a hundred yards away from the scene of the robbery was the police office, adjoining the entrance gate to the aerodrome, where nothing untoward or suspicious had been noticed. Sometime between 10.00pm and 7.00am (when the gold was delivered and the loader arrived to collect it), a car had driven up to the building and the thieves had walked into the aerodrome unchallenged. They had entered the strongroom, removed the gold and driven away into the night.

The most mysterious feature of the baffling case was that although the door to the strongroom safe was found open, it had not been forced. There were only two keys to the safe and both had been accounted for. Police were adamant that it was an impossibility that any person could obtain a sufficiently accurate impression of the keys to open the door. Prior to going into the strongroom, the gold had been under constant watch in the freight department. The strongroom door was removed by the police in order that it could be examined closely by a locksmith. By the following day, a reward of £2,000 was offered for information leading to the safe return of the stolen gold, with two assessors acting for the owners offering £1,000 each.

Special Branch had officers on duty around all ports, having been asked by Scotland Yard to make inquiries about any suspicious people with doubtful passports coming into Britain. At the same time, the Flying Squad were instructed to make enquiries in the known haunts of London criminals, with a view to tracing the movements of Continental and/or British thieves. The haul had proved to be around one-third of the total £60,000 worth of gold destined for Europe.

There was then a dramatic twist in the story when, on 8th March, following inquiries, a man was taken to Croydon police station and questioned in connection with the loss of the gold. The police investigation, headed by Superintendent Helby and Divisional Inspector Detective Widdocks of Croydon police, scoured north London in an endeavour to trace a young blonde woman and three men whom they were anxious to interview in connection with the robbery. The woman had been seen with four men in a car shortly before midnight on the night in question, and police believed they had their first clue when a man changed two new £1 notes in a Holloway pub. The notes had consecutive numbers and it was ascertained that they had been paid to the man by a jeweller for some sovereigns.

Following this, the police visited a house in Kentish Town, where they discovered charred wood resembling the boxes in which the gold had been housed and a skeleton key. The key was taken by Helby to Croydon Aerodrome, where it was discovered that it fitted the strongroom door and could lock and unlock the entrance. At this stage, the police were confident that the gold was still in north London and widened their net in the area. This led the authorities to 47-year-old artist Cecil Swanland, of no fixed abode, who was charged in connection with the missing gold.

At his hearing, Swanland – who was believed to have been working alongside three other men (not in custody) – was remanded in custody having said that he had nothing to say when formal evidence was given. He was charged with complicity in the gold robbery. Two days later, on 12th March, a second man was arrested in Croydon after being questioned at the local police station. He was due to appear at Croydon Police Court that morning, after staff from the aerodrome identified him in a line-up at the station yard.

On 19th March, three men – including Swanland – were charged with theft of the gold in connection with others. Standing beside the artist were Silvio Mazzarda, a commissions agent, and John O'Brien, a dealer of stolen goods. Prosecuting, Mr Graham Brooks said that a female witness, Mrs Lauri Sholz, who was Swanland's landlady, had been threatened in the street not to give evidence against the three men. It was reported that a man named Francis Johnson, who had one of the keys to the strongroom, had been on duty at the aerodrome at the time of the robbery. He had been the only man there and at 4.15am was called to receive a German aeroplane. He was gone from his post for about 45 minutes. Meanwhile, at 1.00am a north London taxi driver was woken by a man he knew as "Little Harry". Three other men (one of whom was called "Shonk") were taken by taxi alongside Little Harry to the corner of Purley Way. At 4.45am, the four men got out of the taxi and walked towards Croydon Aerodrome – by this time, Johnson was on the landing ground – and they returned in a small black car from which they transferred three heavy boxes into the taxi. They told the driver it was gold and he asked them to remove it from his cab, but the four men refused. Shonk then drove away in the black car and the taxi driver took the three remaining men and the gold to Pemberton Road in Harringay, where Swanland had been lodging.

Mrs Scholz had been woken by the sound of heavy banging coming from Swanland's room, as if something were being broken up. Looking out of her bedroom window, she was able to see clouds of smoke coming out of Swanland's room and, at 7.50am, the chimney caught fire. The following evening, Mrs Scholz saw her lodger leaving the premises with a suitcase. It was there that the police found the skeleton key – made of wire – which fitted the lock of the inner door of the strongroom. Swanland's pockets were found to contain a document bearing the name and address of the wife of a pilot from Imperial Airways, although there was no suggestion that the woman knew Swanland or had any connection to the case.

George Manson, the taxi driver, was called to the witness box and identified Mazzarda as the man he knew as "Shonk". He had picked up the men at King's Cross before driving them to Purley Way, but he was unsure about any of the other men who had got into his cab that night. By 26th March, Manson was viewed as a hostile witness and was closely cross-examined by the prosecution when the case came before the magistrates again. The three men in the dock – Swanland, 38-year-old Mazzarda and 74-year-old O'Brien – were sent for trial. However, Manson then told the court that he couldn't remember signing a statement at Croydon police station after the identity parade – where he'd picked out Mazzarda as the man he knew as "Shonk". Asked if Mazzarda was the man who drove the small black car up to the taxi from the direction of the aerodrome, Manson replied: "I don't remember." Manson was asked by the court if he'd lost his memory. However, Mrs Lauri Sholz had been offered protection by the court when she had been threatened to keep her mouth shut, and all three men on trial were refused bail.

The following month, the court was filled with a conversation said to have taken place in Brixton Prison and the acquittal of one of the three accused. The jury found O'Brien not guilty and he was discharged. The court recorder, Mr R F Colam, KC, stated that the only evidence against O'Brien was that of George Manson and that the conviction would not be safe. The prosecutor, Graham Brooks, then told the court that another man named Steel, who was waiting trial in Brixton Prison, had the duty of delivering newspapers to prisoners on remand. Steel had read about the gold robbery and the arrest of Swanland who was at that time on remand in Brixton. Steel reportedly spoke to Swanland and said: "That is a smart job you have pulled off at Croydon," and got the reply: "Yes, but somebody's double-crossed us, and they found some seals."

When Manson was again cross-examined by Hector Hughes, KC, defending Mazzarda, and asked if "Shonk" had anything to do with the crime, the taxi driver's reply was: "Nothing at all." Mr Hughes continued: "Before the identification parade, did the police show you a photograph of Mazzarda and say, 'That is Shonk's photographs, and we want you to identify Shonk'?" Manson replied: "Yes." The hearing was then adjourned.

Both O'Brien and Silvio Mazzarda were found not guilty and discharged. However, Swanland was given a sentence of seven years' penal servitude at Croydon Quarter Sessions on 29th April 1935. Swanland had already had seven previous convictions against him; five of which involved penal servitude. Passing sentence, the recorder told Swanland: "It strikes me that you are a very dangerous man." In his defence, the accused denied that he broke into the aerodrome or took away the gold. He saw a man whom he knew as Little Harry and a taxi at Manor Gate in Harringay. He told the court that up against the seat of the cab and partly covered by a raincoat were three wooden boxes of which the lids were in pieces. He said that Little Harry told him someone had thrown the boxes into the taxi and he took them from his acquaintance in good faith.

At today's prices, the gold, which was never recovered, is worth around £12 million. Despite being a member (and getaway driver) of the notorious Sabini gang, Mazzarda had walked away from the crime due to the police handling of the identification parade. He was interviewed again in 1937 when he told police that the copies of the strongroom keys had been obtained from Burtwell Peters, the chief unloader at the aerodrome. Police came to believe that the gold was eventually transported to 48 Dean Street, London, where Mrs Swanland lived with her mother after her husband's custodial sentence and their eviction from the home they had lodged in with Lauri Sholz. Despite having no income, the former artist's wife was known to have had a substantial bank account after the robbery.

Eastcastle Street

(1952)

The attention of Scotland Yard was centred in May 1952 on the question of "who is the tip-off man" that enables a highly organized gang of mailbag robbers to strike only when "high value" mail is in transit? On 21st May that year, a raid was carried out by seven masked men wearing silk scarves and handkerchiefs, who beat up a GPO van-crew of three and got away with registered mail worth more than £44,500. The haul, in a quiet street off London's Oxford Street, brought about a net sum of more than £91,500 taken during three major unsolved mail robberies.

A special investigation got under way once there had been questions answered as to the carriage and transit of registered postal packets, and the postmaster general ordered to tighten all post office security arrangements. A statement on the robbery was given in the Houses of Parliament on 22nd May 1952. Senior police officials and GPO investigators noted that each time the mail robbers – known as the "Tip-Off Boys" – acted, they focused their attentions on registered mail containing Bank of England notes in bulk, which was generally being transferred from business firms who do not keep check of the identification numbers on the notes. Most of the mail stolen in the third raid was addressed to firms in Hatton Garden, the centre of Britain's diamond industry. The gang were believed to have got away with thousands of pounds worth of uncut diamonds – one of the safest, most negotiable "currencies" (alongside stolen goods and soiled Treasury notes). Attempts to catch up with the gang had been ongoing for six years, but little had been heard of the "Tip-Off Boys" since their last big robbery in 1950 when they managed to steal jewellery worth around £14,000.

The two guards badly beaten in the Eastcastle Street robbery, postmen Rogers and Syms, were treated at Middlesex Hospital for their injuries sustained in the attack. Both men had been dragged from the van along with their driver, Johnson, before being beaten with iron bars and coshes. Meanwhile, fingerprint experts were examining the van door in an attempt to find clues as to the gang's identity. The ambush had been carefully laid; the van had been "sandwiched" between two cars before it was robbed. Police were desperate not only to catch the gang, but also their tip-off man in the post office who told them when valuable cargoes were being carried.

The gang had also targeted a mailbag on a Manchester to London train, before carrying out a robbery on a Brighton to London train. They struck the same train again and, on both occasions, knew exactly which mailbags to take. The robbery on 21st May 1952 bore all the hallmarks of earlier attacks, including careful organization, pre-planning and pre-knowledge of the cargo on board. The GPO van had reached Eastcastle Street at 4.20am when a dark-green saloon car swerved in front of it, blocking the road broadside. The van driver, Johnson, managed to slam on his brakes and stop about two yards from the car. He witnessed four masked men jump out, whereupon one of the robbers signalled to another green car parked at the end of the street. The second car raced up the street to block the road from behind the van and out jumped three more masked men. The three crew of the GPO van were dragged into the road before being attacked. The mail van was found abandoned later in nearby Albany Street. Forty-six registered packages of "high value" mail were missing, and Hart and Co assessors offered a reward of £4,500 for information about the robbery.

On 23rd May 1952, the biggest crime-hunt in Britain's history was under way to find the men, who had in fact stolen much more than was originally thought. Postmaster General Earl De La Warr told parliament that the haul was believed to total £200,000, but it was soon learned that the final amount was nearer £250,000. New and secret means of beating the mailbag robbers were being studied by the postmaster general and high-ranking police officials in the days following the robbery, and a sizeable reward of £14,500 was offered for information leading to the capture of the London gang. The reward brought out a large number of "squealers" – many of them old lags – who began approaching Scotland Yard's Flying Squad. A number of the informants offered to go "underground" to get information and leads on the gang of seven men, who were still believed to be in their London hideout with their haul. There were just three clues in the hunt. The first was a raincoat left behind at the scene of the crime with a laundry mark "2D 662 C 19", which resulted in police officers scouring London's dry-cleaners and laundries. The second clue was a pair of giant bolt-cutters dropped by the gang. They were identified as having been made by C and J Hampton Ltd in Sheffield, who said they could have been obtained from one of three firms they supplied in the area (of course, the cutters could have been stolen). The final clue was a black mask made out of an old waistcoat of worsted material that was also dropped and left at the scene of the crime.

Police were trying to find out why the alarm bell in the mail van did not work, and believed that one of the gang's accomplices, who knew the planned movements of the van and the method of the alarm, may have disconnected the bell before the van reached Paddington Station. Post office workers were asked at the sorting office whether or not they saw anyone acting suspiciously near the mail van before it left for the station to pick up its intended load. The second car used by the robbers was found on 22nd May in Rose Street in Covent Garden, around 250 yards from Bow Street police station and close to the spot where the first car had been found abandoned on the Wednesday night of the robbery. One mystery was how the second car had managed to stay "lost" while being parked so close to a police station in central London – with the whole of the Metropolitan Police looking for it and every police officer in possession of the car's registration number.

Meanwhile, post office workers were loathe to be armed with guns in an attempt to deter further attacks or robberies, and officials decided against using this as an anti-bandit measure. However, it was decided that there would be greater co-operation with the police and some post office vans were to have escorts travelling in cars when a particularly valuable load was being transported. The drivers and guards of these vans were expected to remain unaware that they were, in fact, being escorted; the Post Office was also considering ordering a number of steel-lined vans, which would defy any would-be robbers for at least a few hours. The Post Office was fast becoming aware that their usual safety measures were simply not good enough to protect their staff or prevent a repeat of the vicious robbery. Feelings were running high that they were dealing with a new type of criminal, one who was more intelligent and daring. Meanwhile, Assistant Commissioner Ronald Howe of the Metropolitan Police was put in charge of the investigation.

He was asked by the home secretary to do all that he could to track down the gang. Chief Superintendent Bill Chapman ("The Cherub") and Chief Inspector Bob Lea, both heads of the Flying Squad, briefed their squads of detectives for action. The group of police officials, which also included "undercover" women detectives, were told to look for men aged around 20 years old – possibly ex-borstal boys – who had records for robbery with violence. They were also asked to look out for expert drivers who may have been describing themselves as barrow boys or "dealers". Scotland Yard believed at the time that the gang may have women accomplices who were "hiding" them, and that the men involved were possibly carrying out their usual jobs and routines in order not to arouse suspicion through unexplained absences.

Further to the investigation, detectives were also still desperately trying to find out what had happened on a London to Manchester parcel train that same week, where it was believed that the mailbags had been tampered with before they left London. Porters found 11 parcels ripped open when the 4.00am train from Marylebone arrived at Manchester. Added to this, it seemed that other would-be thieves were joining in the act when a "top secret" alarm at a post office in Small Heath, Birmingham, foiled robbers hoping to gain entry by cutting through the roof of the building.

The headlines in the *Daily Mirror* on 13th June 1952 asked readers "Where do YOU think it is hidden?". It had been 23 days since the robbery, and seven masked mail robbers were still sitting tight on £250,000. Not a trace of the haul (in £1 and £10 notes) had been found, even though the amount stolen would be difficult to hide: the money would easily fill three tea-chests, or six very large suitcases. The *Daily Mirror* asked readers where they would look for the money if they were in charge of the police investigation. The newspaper also revealed that there was so much money involved that it would take a trained bank cashier two days to count the notes, which could cover 12 tennis courts, two ice rinks or one-third of the ground floor at the Bank of England. The money couldn't be spent for the time being and it couldn't be banked, so where was it?

Police forces across the country had failed to find the missing money, despite their best endeavours, vast experience and ingenuity. Suspect homes in several districts of London had been searched. Detectives had stripped down cocktail cabinets, tapped hot-water tanks, pulled up floorboards and examined garage floors for signs of new cement; and the Flying Squad and patrol police had taken thousands of statements. But, the treasure hunt continued with a 24-hour watch on seaports, airfields and any location where money could pass freely, including racetracks, pubs and West End restaurants. The investigation even extended to Eire and France. The *Daily Mirror* asked its readers to think about any bright or new ideas they might have that might lead the police to find the loot. It stated: "That quarter of a million stays hidden. Perhaps YOU can help because this is a treasure hunt without clues, and it needs brainwave ideas. A reader may produce a theory that could set off a new line of inquiry."

One of the problems facing the police was that if they were dealing with a "new type" of criminal, it was entirely possible that the gang involved didn't have police records. If so, then this made house-to-house enquiries difficult, because this method of investigation often centred around those with a criminal record. Police believed that if one member of the gang were picked up then the others would follow. However, at that point, all they had to aid them in their quest was one raincoat, bolt-cutters and a mask. The police thought it unlikely that any of the gang would hide the loot in their own homes. If caught, the robbers were going to want to find freedom with their ill-gotten gains after leaving prison, so hiding the money anywhere obvious was probably not the answer. The police did consider whether or not the gang had hidden the money in a sealed tank (perhaps in a river) but quickly dismissed the idea when they realized just how large the tank would need to be. They also considered whether or not the gang's leader might be calmly hanging on to the money in the boot of a large car; however, anyone following this option would have to be confident that if the gang were rounded up, he would remain at liberty. The police thought this unlikely, too. So where could it be? Had the money been buried in a random back garden while the occupants of the house were away? An Essex weekend gardener might have had £10,000 of uncut diamonds under his vegetable patch but didn't know anything about it until the police uncovered the haul and dug it up. Could the money be hidden in a wood or on a moor? This seemed implausible, however, given that the spade work involved would show for the next 10 years. Had the gang travelled north? Had they gone abroad? The *Daily Mirror* put all these questions to its readership. The prize, of course, was £14,500 being offered as a reward by the assessors.

The loss of so much money – so easily – had shocked the Home Office and it was thought likely that the safety of the Crown jewels should be considered. The jewels – thus far considered burglar-proof in their Tower of London stronghold – are periodically taken to the Bank of England and to a secret address in London's West End for cleaning. But the Home Office declared that it needed to ensure that the safety precautions taken on these journeys were sufficient. Meanwhile, Scotland Yard were no nearer to tracking down the robbers, and no information had been forthcoming in relation to any of the clues, except from a laundress in Liverpool who believed that the laundry mark on the raincoat could have come from a ship's laundry, with the "C" standing for cabin and the "D" for deck.

In September 1952, George King (known as two-gun Ginger) died in Pentonville Prison at the age of 28. Serving 12 years for his part with seven masked men in a £6,000 mail van hold-up in north London, he was known to Scotland Yard as one of the country's toughest bandits and was suspected to have known the identity of the gang. However, the heart condition from which he was suffering finally got the better of him – and the young man took his secrets with him to the grave. As King was on remand in Brixton Prison at the time of the £250,000 robbery, the police knew he hadn't taken part in it. However, they were convinced that he knew who the gang were – and went to visit him in prison to talk to him about the heist. The renowned robber kept his mouth firmly closed during questioning and refused to give the police any information. His death seemed to signal the end of the investigation for the police and, as a result, the money and the gang remained out of reach.

The gang was led by London gangster Billy Hill (1911–84) but neither he, nor his gang, were ever caught. Terry "Lucky Tel" Hogan was a member of the gang and was just 20 years old when he robbed the mail van in 1952. He had been recruited by Billy Hill at a time when most of Britain's crime followed a "smash and grab" culture, but Hill had a completely new approach to robbery. He pioneered "project" crimes that were meticulously planned, and in which the gang members were mentored and taught secrecy and loyalty. Despite newspaper reports that the amount stolen totalled £250,000, the gang actually got away with £287,000 (around £6.5 million in today's money).

Terry "Lucky Tel" Hogan was not your average underworld criminal, however, and spent his early years in prison reading as much as he could in order to educate himself. He had come from a dysfunctional family and was not prepared for his children to suffer the same way he did. He was well known and highly respected within the circles he moved in. Yet although he did go on to take part in further robberies, he wanted no part in the "Great Train Robbery" of 1963. Just 10 months earlier, in November 1962, the Flying Squad at Scotland Yard had failed to intercept the robbery of an armoured truck payroll shipment at Heathrow Airport. Terry Hogan was part of the gang that netted £62,000 (around £950,000 in today's money). The robbery was well-planned and meticulously executed, with Lucky Tel being responsible for ensuring that the money and the other gang members were able to get away from the scene of the crime. The escape was via two stolen Jaguars, driven by Roy James – a racing driver and part-time "cat burglar" – and Micky Ball, who was eventually arrested and served five years for the crime. However, the jury failed to reach a verdict on the involvement of 32-year-old Douglas Goody.

Derek Bentley and Christopher Craig

(1952)

In a packed courtroom in Croydon, Surrey, a youth of 19 denied that he took part in the murder of a policeman shot dead during a rooftop battle in Croydon on Sunday, 2nd November 1952. The charge against Derek William Bentley, from Fairview Road, Norbury, alleged that he was concerned with Christopher Craig (then aged 16) in murdering Constable Sidney Miles, a radio-car driver with 22 years' service in the police force. At the time of the case, Craig was in Croydon General Hospital with detectives at his bedside, where he was suffering from fractured ribs and a fractured wrist sustained during a fall.

According to Chief Detective Inspector John Smith, Bentley alleged after his arrest that Craig fired the shot that killed Constable Miles. The detective had seen Bentley at 5.30am on the morning of 3rd November to tell him that he would be charged with being concerned in the murder. Bentley was then remanded in custody and offered legal aid. The young man asked instead for his father. Mr Bentley senior arranged legal aid for his son and was allowed to see him. Meanwhile, another officer, 37-year-old Detective Constable Frederick Fairfax, who was wounded in the shoulder during the shooting, was allowed out of hospital. Five policemen, it was said, had shown "calm courage" on a warehouse roof on the cloudy and wet November night when 42-year-old Constable Miles was killed.

According to the prosecution, Fairfax clambered up a drainpipe to the roof and was shot in the shoulder as Bentley and Craig tried to escape after an attempted robbery at a confectionery warehouse. The two would-be robbers had been spotted climbing up the drainpipe of the warehouse by a girl in a house opposite. After she'd alerted her parents, the girl's father went to the nearest telephone box and called the police. Fairfax was able to arrest Bentley and later went back on the roof with a revolver to face Craig. Miles kicked open the staircase door to the roof and went fearlessly forward before being shot between the eyes by 16-year-old Craig. Constable Harrison was forced to retreat along the gutter beside a sloping roof and followed Miles up the staircase, where he hurled his truncheon, a milk bottle and a block of wood at Craig. Constable McDonald tried twice to climb the drainpipe to help Fairfax, and Constable Jacks also reached the roof by the drainpipe. Craig was alleged to have told the police: "If I hadn't cut a bit off the barrel of my gun [so it would fit inside his pocket], I would probably have killed a lot more policemen. That night I was out to kill because I had so much hate inside me for what they had done to my brother." David Nelson, acting for Craig, told magistrates that there might be a question about Craig's mental state.

As the case continued, Craig was brought to court on a stretcher to hear the policemen's side of the story. Fairfax, upon climbing the drainpipe, had seen Bentley and Craig standing about 15 yards in front of him. They then backed behind the lift shaft and the police officer got within 6ft of the two youths before telling them to come out. One of the teenagers shouted: "If you want us ... well come and get us."

Fairfax went behind the stack and grabbed Bentley, pulling him out. Craig exited the opposite side. At this point, Bentley broke away and shouted: "Let him have it, Chris." Fairfax was then shot by Craig. There was a further shot and Fairfax and Bentley lay on the ground. Fairfax found a knuckle-duster and a knife on Bentley – both of which had been given to him by Craig – and was told by the young man: "That's all I've got, gov'nor, I have not got a gun." Craig was asked to drop his gun but replied: "Come and get it." Bentley then said: "He has got a 45 Colt and plenty of ammunition for it, too." At this point, Miles burst through the door of the staircase and was shot by Craig. Following this, Fairfax armed himself and shouted to Craig: "Drop your gun. I also have a gun." He was told by Craig: "Come on then, copper, let's have it out." After Fairfax was shot at again by Craig, he ran in a semi-circular direction towards the young man, firing two shots as he went. Craig vanished over the roof.

On 10th December 1952, both Bentley and Craig were due in the witness box at the Old Bailey. Meanwhile, in court, the jury heard how drugs had been given to Craig before an operation on his wrist, including pentothal, sometimes referred to as the "truth drug" because of its abilities to "undermine the will and make people talk much more freely and say things they would not normally say". However, when questioned, Dr Gordon Hadfield confirmed that the dose had been "smallish". By this time, the court had heard how Craig could not read owing to "word-blindness" and that Bentley also had difficulties and was unable to write. However, a police officer did not agree that the youth was feeble-minded. Craig's counsel objected to two women jurors, and two men were brought in to make an all-male jury. Christmas Humphreys, prosecuting, said that the case for the Crown was that Craig wilfully murdered the constable and gloried in the murder. He also stated that Bentley had incited his companion, and that although he was technically under arrest at the time of the murder, he was party to the crime and therefore equally responsible in law. Both teenagers had the support of their families during the trial, and Craig's father denied that his son was violent. In fact, he insisted to the court that his young son was gentle-natured. The jury decided the fate of Craig and Bentley on 11th December 1952.

Crown counsel and defence counsel had addressed the jury for the last time in what had been, according to newspaper reports at the time, a "close-packed" drama. Lord Goddard would carry out the summing up and direct the jury on the law. Craig's counsel, E J Parris had pleaded passionately with the jury to believe that the boy had had no intention of killing Constable Miles and that it had all been a tragic accident. He stated that Craig was a film-struck stupid boy, who saw himself as a "brave crook" and nothing more. According to Craig's defence, he had never meant to kill; he should be found guilty only of manslaughter. However, the prosecution had argued that Craig had shot 10 or 11 times, which meant he had to have reloaded the gun. Thus, the prosecution argued, he had to have known what he was doing.

What also seemed to weigh heavily on the minds of those in court was the fact that Craig had expressed no remorse for his actions – until questioned about it twice by the judge, when Craig then said that he was sorry for what he had done. When Derek Bentley gave evidence, he denied that he had told Craig to use the gun on the police officers. Bentley said how he had seen Craig on the morning of the shooting but that no arrangement had been made about what would happen later. He said that when they had got on the bus from Norbury to Croydon he didn't know that they were going to break in anywhere. On the bus, Craig gave him the knuckleduster but he was unaware that his companion had a gun in his pocket. They had looked in the window of a sweet shop and Craig had climbed over an iron fence without saying anything. Bentley had followed. Once on the roof, someone shone a light from a garden and they hid behind a stack. Bentley said he made no attempt to struggle or strike when Fairfax got hold of him. He also said that Fairfax did not hold on to him once under arrest, and that there had been nothing to stop him from joining Craig if he had wanted to. He said that in the police car he had told police officers the name of the man on the roof. He did not say that he knew Craig had a gun but that he didn't think he'd use it. He also stressed that he did not at any time tell Craig to use violence towards the police. The prosecuting counsel had then asked Bentley if that meant that the police were untrue in their stories. When asked, Bentley stated: "We came to break in and not to kill."

Christmas Humphreys was adamant that the court should find the two defendants guilty of murder. However, F H Cassels, acting for Bentley, said to the jury: "If you come to the conclusion that what Craig did was accidental, and thereby find a verdict of manslaughter, then, in my submission, you can't find Bentley guilty of murder." Cassels went on to state that even if Craig was found guilty of murder, the case for Bentley was different: "He did not fire the shot." He also told the court how Bentley had at no time shown any violence or resistance to the police, and if he was being accused of inciting Craig to use violence then his behaviour was unusual. When discussing the words: "Let him have it, Chris", Cassels asked the jury to consider a different interpretation to the one given, whereby Bentley was accused of inciting Craig to fire at the police. He argued that Bentley could have been pleading with his friend to let the police officers take charge of the weapon. He concluded his 35-minute address by telling the jury: "You can convict Bentley only if you are satisfied that he knew Craig had the gun, and incited Craig to use it."

On 11th December 1952, Derek William Bentley – just 19 years old – was sentenced to death at the Old Bailey. He had been found guilty, alongside Christopher Craig, of the murder of Constable Miles. Craig was ordered to be detained at Her Majesty's pleasure. Bentley, however, faced hanging. The jury, finding him guilty of murder, recommended him to mercy; the home secretary had to decide on the young man's fate. The official attitude was defined in a memorandum sent to the Royal Commission on Capital Punishment, which read: "The Home Secretary always attaches weight to a recommendation to mercy by the jury. He would be very reluctant to disregard such a recommendation if it is concurred by the Judge." But, the judge, Lord Chief Justice Goddard, was firm in his belief that the police deserved special protection in the execution of their duties and that anyone killing a police officer was guilty of murder. It also transpired that 16-year-old Norman Parsley pleaded guilty to armed robbery at the Old Bailey, which the court had no doubt he had committed with Christopher Craig. In fact, Craig had given Parsley the gun. Craig's brother, Niven, age 26 – whom Christopher idolized – had already been sentenced to 12 years for armed robbery; hence Craig's anger on the night of the murder of Constable Miles.

The conviction of Christopher Craig was the second time in two months that the Craig family heard that two of their children were "dangerous". Niven had been a cherished son who had won a scholarship to grammar school, but after falling in with the wrong crowd he began getting into more and more trouble. Christopher had grown up in an environment where his older brother brought disrepute to the family. He followed in his brother's footsteps and had a growing fascination with guns.

At the beginning of 1953, home secretary, Sir David Maxwell Fyfe, faced the difficult decision as to whether or not Derek Bentley would hang. Bentley's appeal had already been dismissed, and the time and date for the execution were pending. There were a number of factors that kept the country guessing as to the 19-year-old's fate. Would Sir David listen to the jury's recommendation for mercy? Would he take the youngster's age into account and the fact that he wasn't carrying a gun nor did he fire the shots? Bentley's appeal had been dismissed by three judges at the Law Courts in London and, by this time, Sir David had decided not to reprieve the young man. However, the question of whether or not the youth should be executed resulted in an 11th-hour fight for his life in a debate in the Commons just 12 hours before he was due to hang on 28th January 1953. Some 200 MPs were intent on persuading the home secretary that he had made the wrong decision. Even the judge at the trial believed that Bentley's guilt was less than Craig's; and it seemed that the jury's plea for mercy was being ignored. The home secretary said he had given careful consideration to the last-ditch petition arguing for clemency in a letter to the Commons, but that he could find no reason to revise his decision.

Derek Bentley's family visited him in Wandsworth Prison on 27th January 1953 for the last time. His father, William Bentley, told newspaper reporters that it hadn't been all tears and that his son had been "cheerful, even under the shadow of the gallows". Mr Bentley senior had urged that evidence on his son's mental condition should have been given at the trial. Bentley had suffered severe head injuries during a bombing raid in the Second World War, which had caused the family home to collapse around him; this event had compounded an earlier injury he'd suffered at the age of four when he fell 15ft from a lorry and hit his head on the pavement. This earlier injury had caused the young man to develop epilepsy, which led to a series of health and developmental problems that had dogged him for his entire life. None of this evidence was heard in court and, arguably, Bentley did not receive a fair trial as a result. Although 19 years old, Bentley was probably younger mentally than Craig.

At 9.00am on 28th January 1953, Derek Bentley was hanged for murder.

In March 1962, it was reported that Craig might be released from prison when he was moved from Wormwood Scrubs to the open prison at Leyhill in Gloucestershire. The prison, known for its rehabilitation course, was often where prisoners soon to be released were sent prior to starting a life outside prison walls. Craig was eventually released in May 1963.

In 1966, the Bentley family were allowed to remove Derek Bentley's body from Wandsworth Prison so that he could be buried in a family grave with a proper burial. The body of Bentley was reburied in Croydon Cemetery on 4th March 1966, where nine family members attended a service in his memory. However, the story didn't end there for the family, who fought to prove the innocence of their lost son.

After 38 years, the idea of a pardon for Derek Bentley was mooted in the press in 1991, when it was discovered that the then home secretary, Kenneth Baker, was to reopen the case. Bentley's sister, Iris, even after the death of both her parents, fought the British Government in order to gain a pardon for her late brother. There had been a number of books, plays and TV commentaries all arguing that Bentley's execution was a grave miscarriage of justice. In September that year, even Christopher Craig told reporters that Bentley had been innocent of murder. He claimed that his friend had tried to get him to hand over the gun to the police; not to use it on them. Craig even went so far as to say that the police withheld vital evidence in the case against Bentley so that he would face the gallows. He claimed that the police deliberately did not reveal that the dead man, who had the mental age of 11, had tried to persuade him to hand over his gun.

In a letter before his death, Bentley wrote to his mother, Lillian, via a member of the prison staff by dictating:

"I tell you what mum the truth of this story has got to come out one day, and as I said in the visiting box that – one day a lot of people are going to get into trouble and I think you know who these people are. What do you think mum?"

These words would return to haunt British justice when the case was reopened by Kenneth Baker: they took on a completely new significance. Since Bentley's death, Iris had laid a wreath at the gates of Wandsworth Prison every year on the anniversary of her brother's death. In 1992, she said: "To get Derek's pardon means everything to me. I know it won't bring him back but it will show the world we have been telling the truth for 39 years." It wasn't until 30th July 1998 that Derek Bentley received a full posthumous pardon when the Court of Appeal quashed his conviction for murder. Sadly, for his parents and his sister, Iris, the pardon came too late for them to witness. Had he lived, Bentley himself would have been 64 years old.

Despite the public outcry over the hanging of a 19-year-old man with a mental age of 11, who did not commit the murder, it took almost 46 years for Derek Bentley to be fully pardoned. The chief public executioner, Albert Pierrepoint, gave a moving account of the convicted youth's final moments. He said: "When you go to hang a boy of 19, it does not matter that he is tall and broad-shouldered. At 9.00am on the morning he is to die, he still looks only a boy." He recalled Bentley's favourite joke: "I have beaten the warders at cards again today, but I still can't beat them to the door."

Eventually, the Bentley family won compensation for the death of Derek. His younger brother Dennis said: "I am delighted the home secretary has decided to make an award, but no amount of money will bring back my brother or erase the pain and suffering my family has experienced."

Great Train Robbery

(1963)

In August 1963, Terry "Lucky Tel" Hogan was sitting on a beach in Cannes in the south of France when news reached him of the Great Train Robbery. Despite his friendships with the likes of Bruce Reynolds and Buster Edwards, Hogan had been reluctant to take part in the £2.6 million heist (£37 million in today's money) due to what he felt were flawed plans and the involvement of too many people. However, he did hide some of the money for a day or so following the robbery of the Glasgow to London mail train.

The robbery was committed on 8th August 1963 at Bridego Railway Bridge, Ledburn, near Mentmore in Buckinghamshire. It was carried out by a gang of 15 men, including the leader Bruce Reynolds, alongside Gordon Goody, Charlie Wilson, Ronald "Buster" Edwards and Roger Cordrey, an electronics expert who was already an accomplished train robber. Ronnie Biggs had a minor role in the heist: to provide the replacement driver. He brought along "Old Pete", who failed at his task when he discovered he was unable to operate the modern locomotive. Two other members of the gang – who acted as informants – were the "Ulsterman" (who has never been identified or caught) and Brian Field.

The train's driver, Jack Mills, had set off from Glasgow Central Station at 6.50pm on 7th August, bound for Euston Station in London, with 12 carriages carrying 72 post office employees who were busy sorting the mail. Much of the mail had been loaded before the train began its journey, but some was collected at stations en route and from line-side collection points where mailbags were elevated on track-side hooks caught by nets from the train itself. The second carriage housed the "high value" registered mail, which was unusually high on this particular journey as Scotland had just enjoyed a bank-holiday weekend. The train was brought to a stop by a red signal light, which the gang had engineered. The train's second man, David "Dave" Whitby, was sent down from the engine to contact the signalman, but found that the wires had been cut. Meanwhile, members of the gang, wearing balaclavas, were shouting and running along the railway line. The driver watched as the third carriage was uncoupled from the train and, after putting up a fight, was coshed over the head with an iron bar wrapped in cloth. He had little choice but to drive the train forwards as instructed, while the gang broke into the two coaches holding the money. They ordered five sorting staff into a corner and threatened them. The driver had moved the train forwards about a mile before he was ordered to stop by one of the gang who had been peering out of the cab, apparently looking for the stopping place. Jack Mills could see that his train had stopped near a white canvas sheet stretched between two poles beside the line. About 15 men were waiting by the marker and as the train stopped they all jumped on board. The men, wearing dark boiler suits with masked faces, then ordered the driver and the train's second man, Dave Whitby, to get out of the cab, where they were handcuffed together and forced to lie face down on the grass verge beside the line. Around 100 mailbags were swiftly unloaded from the train (not taking more than a few minutes) and into a waiting lorry. Mills was, by now, bleeding heavily from his head wound, and was threatened with more of a beating should he or Dave make any movement or call for help. Five minutes later, the two handcuffed men heard the lorry engine revving up and then all was quiet.

Meanwhile, further up the track, it had become so quiet that the other coaches back at Sears Crossing began to wonder what was going on. The guard, 61-year-old Tom Miller, thought that the train had broken down. He left the train and walked a mile back down the track to warn other trains of the danger. He was surprised on returning to the train to see that the front two coaches and the engine had gone. He tried to telephone from the boxes along the line, but also found that the wires had been cut so he set out to walk to Cheddington, two miles away, en route stumbling across the engine and the two front coaches. He found his handcuffed colleagues and stopped a goods train, asking the driver to look after them before making his way, once again, towards Cheddington. He called the police and requested an ambulance to attend to his driver and three postal workers who had also been coshed by the gang. The two drivers, still handcuffed together, were taken to the Royal Bucks Hospital in Aylesbury, where Jack Mills required eight stitches to his head wound and firemen were called to cut the handcuffs (although a local policeman was able to free them with a key).

The authorities quickly established that the gang had expert knowledge of trains: they had managed to uncouple the train and obviously had someone capable of driving the train should they have needed to. The robbery on the travelling post office was the ninth major train robbery in the south of England over a three-year period. Billed in the press as the "Greatest Train Robbery", Scotland Yard officials agreed that there had never been anything quite so big, bold and crookedly brilliant. The heist, quite simply, had been one of the most amazing ambushes ever known. When the crew had seen the signal light showing an amber warning, there had been nothing to show that anything especially unusual was happening. There was nothing to show that the signal was faked, that telephone lines in the area had been cut or that a gang of 15 ruthless men were lying in wait. There had been nothing to suggest to 58-year-old Mills and 26-year-old Whitby that they were about to become victims in the biggest, boldest robbery in British history. Mills had braked as he saw the fake red light, and the train had rolled to a standstill near the road bridge at Sears Crossing.

The travelling post office usually had three bandit-proof vans, but between 22nd June and 2nd August 1963 all were out of action, so were not available on the night of the robbery. Police began investigating why two of the vans had "hot axles" that were in danger of seizing up due to faulty bearings, and why the third had a wheel rim worn down. The vans were taken to Wigan, Swindon and Derby respectively, but none were ready in time for the Glasgow to London run after the bank holiday. As a result, three new plans were unveiled by the postmaster general, including security men travelling with valuable cargos, greater co-operation between signalmen and police and a loud-hailer system. The idea of guards carrying arms was quickly dismissed.

Meanwhile, detectives studied reports that a small private plane took off at dawn from a deserted airfield just a few miles from the hold-up spot, with police believing that the ambush ringleaders had hidden their loot and escaped from the UK. A reward of £260,000 – tax free – was offered to anyone leading the police to the return of the money and catching of the gang members. Hart and Co, and Topliss and Hardy, acting for the seven banks hit by the raid, were offering at least £200,000 of the reward, while Midland Bank offered a further £50,000 and the Post Office £10,000.

Just four days after the robbery, police were working on a hunch that the money and the gang were hiding within 20 miles of the crime scene, seeing as roadblocks were set up within 60 minutes of the ambush and the gang would only have had a 50-minute head start before the alarm was raised; it would have taken them 90 minutes to reach London down the M1, where their two lorries and a jeep would have been easily visible to the police hunting for them. All newly bought or rented houses in the area were being checked; hundreds of phone calls came in from members of the public seeking a share in the reward money; and 70 police dogs swept across the countryside near Sears Crossing looking in farms, barns and cottages. Police forces in Bedfordshire, Hertfordshire and Oxfordshire were warned that the gang could be hiding in their area.

Jack Mills, photographed in the newspaper with his head bandaged, stated that he felt the gang would have killed him if he hadn't been important to their plans. He said of the robbers' ambush: "It was a fantastic operation, timed with military precision ... it was done in almost complete silence and everyone seemed to know what he had to do, and did it." He went on to say that he was confident that the gang had railway knowledge, but that: "I'm certain they didn't know how to drive the diesel ... and that's what saved me."

The telephones at the offices of Hart and Co, the City of London loss adjusters and insurance assessors, just didn't stop ringing. And neither did the succession of callers with private business to the firm's Lawrence Lane offices in EC2. Despite the estimated 67 per cent crank calls, no one was turned away in the hunt for information. Informants came forward with the names of dodgy men staying in boarding houses, to the name of every known criminal in London and even a man who kept a note of the comings and goings at his cafe in Buckinghamshire. All information was passed to Scotland Yard to be followed up as appropriate, including the theory that the money had been stowed on a barge that was spirited down the Grand Union Canal while police resources were concentrating their efforts on watching the roads. Then came the news that Clydesdale Bank had also lost out during the robbery to the tune of £95,000.

On 13th August 1963, police were led to a remote farm and experts were brought in to examine clues. Leatherslade Farm, in Oakley, suddenly became the centrepiece of the investigation for Detective Superintendent Malcolm Fewtrell of Bucks CID and Detective Superintendent Gerald McArthur of Scotland Yard when it was discovered that it had been used as a hideout for the gang. A Land Rover and a lorry were left behind at the scene, where it was believed the gang had intended to bury their loot. An incomplete pit was dug to the rear of the farmhouse but it seemed to police that the gang had fled in a hurry.

On 15th August, police announced that they were holding five men in connection with the robbery and then put a total "blackout" for 24 hours on any news of their next moves. Two men were held in Bournemouth, a blonde housewife was arrested in London, and a man and his wife were picked up in East Molesey, Surrey. All five prisoners were taken to the police station in Aylesbury, the headquarters of the investigation. Meanwhile, Flying Squad chief, Detective Chief Superintendent Millen, briefed his nine teams (of almost 100 men) to visit a number of houses around London in a search for nine more suspected men. All officers were banned from giving vital information over the police wavelength in case any of the robbers were listening in: all communication had to be made by telephone. The woman in Bournemouth, who had given the police the tip-off about the two men she believed to be involved in the Great Train Robbery, was moved out of the area by police for fear of reprisals from other gang members. All five prisoners were in possession of large sums of money. The gang also lost a further £100,900 of the loot when it was found abandoned in a Surrey wood at the hillside beauty spot of Redlands, between Dorking and Coldharbour. Two holdalls and a large briefcase were found under trees by two colleagues on a motorbike while on their way to work. Following the discovery, police believed that the big share-out of the money had taken place just a few days before when the gang fled from their Leatherslade Farm hideout in Oakley.

In Bournemouth, a woman named Betty Last was alarmed to hear fighting outside her home in Tweedale Road and called the police. The police were already on the scene, however, having been alerted by another woman, Ethel Clark, who had become suspicious after her tenant William Boal paid three months rent in advance in used notes. Boal was providing a hideout for gang member Roger Cordrey, who was the first of the criminals to be arrested. It was Brian Field's money that was found in the woods in Surrey and it was only a matter of time before the police could prove it.

"Banknote Farm" – as the hideout in Oakley became known – had been bought by the gang some two months prior to the robbery. Police took the place apart over three days, bit by bit. Field had paid £560 deposit to the farm's owner, Bernard Rixon, and had collected the keys, but nothing more was ever heard of him. When the police arrived at the remote dwelling they found large stocks of tinned food, post office sacks, sleeping bags and other camping equipment, along with the vehicles the robbers had used in the heist. There were more than 100 tins of baked beans, corned beef and condensed milk, plus stocks of tea, sugar, coffee and beer, as well as toilet rolls and cooking gear. The stash also included a first-aid kit and eating utensils, which police believed came from a large shop in the London area. There was even a tea strainer, and the police were convinced that a woman, or women, were also involved with the gang as that touch was too dainty to have come from hardened criminals on the run. The provisions ran to more than 170 eggs, plus loaves of bread and slabs of cake, together with sauces and bottles of meat extract.

By this time, four of London's most hardened criminals were at the top of the list of suspects, especially as all the men had been missing from their usual London haunts for more than two weeks. Friends and relatives of the men were questioned, but police met a wall of silence. No one was talking. On 21st August, a further £30,000 of the loot turned up, cleverly hidden in the panelling of an empty caravan at Box Hill in Surrey. The caravan had been bought by two men, one of whom was known to the police. One of the men had returned to the caravan site the following day with a woman, a baby girl and a poodle. The couple took a number of large suitcases inside, and other residents reported hearing quite a bit of disturbance as the couple had hid the loot. At that stage, though, no one had suspected a thing.

On 22nd August, Charlie Wilson was arrested for his part in the robbery at a house in Crescent Lane, Clapham. The following day, police announced that they were looking for 41-year-old Bruce Reynolds and 43-year-old James White. Their pictures were released in the newspapers and more than 75,000 police officers – and now the general public – were looking for them. White was the man police suspected of buying the caravan. Next came pictures of Roy James, known as "The Weasel", who was last seen completing the fastest lap in practice at Goodwood racing circuit at 95.57mph. James failed to appear for practice on 23rd August. Meanwhile, on that same day, police arrested another man – the eighth to be detained – about 60 miles north of Cheddington. Police had also carried out a number of dawn raids on the houses of known criminals, clubs and caravan sites in London and the Home Counties. A restaurant waiter in Italy came forward with news that he believed Reynolds had eaten in his establishment just a few days before. He had asked for a dimly lit table on the terrace for himself and his two companions, before leaving from Follonica, northwest Italy, in a British car.

In a twist in the tale, by the end of the month following the robbery, police believed that many of the robbers had sent their share of the loot by train to hideaways outside London. One of the suspects had bought a heavy wooden packing case, which was packed and nailed shut by three men at a garage in southwest London before being addressed to an engineering firm near Ipswich in Suffolk and sent by train. The hunt was still on for Roy James, while Gordon Goody walked jauntily out of the police station on 25th August, 30 hours after he went inside. Two days later, it was believed that James had gone to Vienna to join a girlfriend. The police handed back Leatherslade Farm to its owner, Bernard Rixon, and Robert Pelham (a 26-year-old motor mechanic from Notting Hill) appeared before Linslade Court in Bucks in connection with the heist charged with receiving £551 of the stolen money.

At the end of August, all police forces were issued with the serial numbers of four-fifths of the fivers stolen in the Great Train Robbery. Since the raid, bank clerks had been working overtime to produce the serial numbers (all 16 pages of them). The police also issued a photograph of Cherry White, the 34-year-old wife of James, who was the woman seen with him at the caravan site in Box Hill. Meanwhile, more than £10,000 in £5 notes had been found at a house in Tolworth, Surrey, and the police were hoping that the serial numbers would match the stolen loot.

The police hunt was still as strong as ever and, on 30th August, they named another man they wanted to talk to in connection with the robbery —John Daly — an Irishman who was believed to be somewhere in Kent with his pregnant wife and baby daughter. But, by early September 1963, the probe switched to Scotland after a female level-crossing keeper, Tillie Montgomery, spotted two couples who police believed could help with their inquiries. Tillie was certain that she had seen Daly and his wife (although the woman's hair looked as if it had been dyed from brunette to fair) at a caravan that had another man and a woman inside. She was fairly sure that the second man was Bruce Reynolds. The two men's wives were sisters so it was not unusual that the two couples would be together, the police surmised. However, an underworld tip-off indicated that both Reynolds and Daly would leave their wives in an instant if they needed to.

On 6th September, press reports covered the story for the first time of builder Ronnie Biggs, 34, who was accused of taking part in the robbery. He told police: "Get on with it. You'll have to prove it all the way. I'm admitting nothing to you people." Biggs of Redhill, Surrey, was the ninth person charged in connection with the crime. He was remanded in custody by magistrates. On 10th September, police announced that they believed Roy James had gone to South America. They also stated that they thought Daly and Reynolds had either had, or were planning to have plastic surgery to alter their appearance. Pictures of the two men had been circulated all over Europe, particularly in Austria, Denmark, Sweden and Germany, where operations by plastic surgeons could be carried out with no questions asked. At this time, the seven men and three women already in custody were again remanded.

Just two days later on 12th September 1963, it was the turn of former London club owner turned florist Buster Edwards, 32, to come under scrutiny by the police, but he was nowhere to be found. His wife and young daughter were also missing and it was believed that the family had travelled to the Continent. Edwards had moved out of the apartment he had shared with his family in Kensington for the past eight years, for no apparent reason, and he had quit his job, leaving his former landlady and boss with no idea where he could have gone. In fact, Edwards turned up in Shepperton for three weeks, where he and his wife were known as Mr and Mrs Green in their new rented accommodation. But when the police arrived at Old Forge Crescent following a call from a neighbour who had seen their pictures on television, it seemed the couple may have been tipped off as the family had simply disappeared.

On 26th September, engineer Roger Cordrey was alleged to have told the police that he was promised a few thousand for his advice on how to stop a mail train. By this point, Brian Field and his boss John Wheater, alongside Lennie Field (no relation), had all been arrested. So, too, had Charlie Wilson, Ronnie Biggs, Jimmy Hussey and Tommy Wisbey. At the court in Aylesbury, Cordrey told the court that he couldn't give them more information or he "would be topped". At this stage, he was one of 13 accused people – 10 men and three women – who sat in a specially built dock in Aylesbury Rural Council chamber for the hearing of 15 charges arising from the robbery. The others in the dock alongside him included William Boal and his wife Renee, plus

Charlie Wilson, Ronnie Biggs, Jimmy Hussey, Tommy Wisbey, Lennie Field, Robert Pelham, Mary Manson, and Alfred Pilgrim and his wife Mary from East Molesey.

The prosecuting counsel told the court of the arrests made so far, the amount of money already retrieved, the planning that had gone into the robbery, how the train driver and post office staff were attacked as they did their jobs, and about the getaway transport used by the thieves. Mr Sabin for the prosecution also went on to describe how the suspects had been caught and apprehended, and how Wilson had been detained after his thumbprints were found on the windowsill at Leatherslade Farm. Buster Edwards' prints were also found at the farm – on a game of Monopoly – while witness Lily Rixon gave evidence and pointed out Lennie Field as one of the men who had come to buy the hideaway farm after it had been advertised for sale. Mr Sabin stated that when Boal was arrested he was found with £57,037 in a holdall, and a pillowcase that contained banknote wrappings, and that he had told police: "Fair enough. It came from the train job." Cordrey also admitted that the money had come from the train robbery but that he was not on the track when the crime was committed.

By the time that solicitor John Wheater, 42, was arrested in mid-October 1963, Gordon Goody was already in custody and 17 people in total were now in the frame. Wheater, who specialized in criminal law, was charged with conspiring with nine other men to stop the mail train with intent to rob, and for harbouring, assisting and maintaining Lennie Field. Brian Field, 29, was the managing clerk at Wheater's firm based in Marble Arch, London. On 18th October, the criminal lawyer was allowed £15,000 bail after denying all charges and being described in court as a "man of good character". Meanwhile, Buster Edwards and his wife June were believed to be hiding out in Norway after the couple came to staff's attention at a hotel when June changed her hair colour from jet-black to vivid red. And, on the day that Wheater denied his knowledge of Lennie Field or the purchase of Leatherslade Farm, police were closing the net on Bob Welch, whose palm print was found on one of the Pipkin beer cans found at the hideaway property. Welch of Islington, north London, was arrested 11 weeks after the robbery and sat in court alongside 18 others accused of involvement. Mr Sabin stated for the court that: "After Welch's prints were taken it was found that his palm print exactly corresponded with a palm print found on the half-full Pipkin."

It transpired that the cans had only been filled and sealed two weeks before the raid, and sent to a brewery in Oxford, whereupon a consignment was then delivered to a shop in Bicester. Ten of the cans were purchased from the shop – just eight miles from the farm – on the day before the robbery. Gordon Goody's shoes were used as evidence against him in court. One of the lorries used in the raid had knocked over a tin of yellow paint – bought to disguise the vehicle following the heist – and then driven through it: upon forensic examination traces of the same paint were found on the soles of Goody's shoes, which were found in a pub at Blackfriars in London. Mixed with the paint on the bottom of Goody's shoes were particles of gravel that had been used to cover over the pool of paint at the farmhouse.

At the beginning of December 1963, detectives swooped on a

flat in a London square and arrested antiques dealer John Daly, who was living with his pregnant wife, Barbara. Daly was escorted – like all the other prisoners – to Aylesbury, where he was charged with conspiring to rob the train. He was the twentieth person to be arrested in connection with the crime. Next came Roy "The Weasel" James, who was arrested on 10th December by Flying Squad detectives before being taken to Cannon Row police station and later transferred to Aylesbury. At this point, Mary Manson had already been cleared of receiving stolen money.

Just a couple of days later, a phone rang at Scotland Yard and a voice said: "Go to the phone box in Great Dover Street and you will find £50,000 in two sacks." Police raced to the scene and found two sacks of banknotes in £1 notes and Scottish £5 notes. When Roy James was arrested he had more than £12,000 in his possession. By this time, the police had recovered more than £275,000 of the £2,600,000 and were confident that they would find the three missing men – Bruce Reynolds, Buster Edwards and James White – who were wanted for questioning. Roy James, meanwhile, was remanded in custody following his 10-minute appearance at Linslade Court.

Towards the end of January 1964, the trial of those accused got under way to a dramatic start when Brian Field's German-born wife, Karen, told how she had been approached by a man asking her to pay £3,000 in order to make jurors at the trial more favourable towards her husband. Mrs Field was actually approached on three occasions prior to the trial and asked for money to ensure that jurors could be influenced. Meanwhile, Roger Cordrey pleaded guilty to conspiring to rob the mail train and to three counts of receiving a total of £140,939. However, he pleaded not guilty to robbery with aggravation. He was taken to prison to await sentencing. Following Mrs Field's evidence in court, the judge ordered that the name of the man who had approached her be written down on a piece of paper, and Mr Justice Edmund Davies eventually ruled that the jury should be sworn in and the trial proceeded.

There were 12 men in the dock, all pleading not guilty to being involved in the Great Train Robbery. Seven other people, including three women, pleaded not guilty to receiving stolen money. The train driver, Jack Mills, gave evidence and told how he hadn't been able to work since the robbery due to his head injuries. The driver was among the first of 200 prosecution witnesses called to the trial, but a twist came on 6th February when an unfortunate and disastrous irregularity concerning the situation with Ronnie Biggs meant that his trial had to be halted after evidence given by Detective Inspector Basil Morris of Reigate. The judge refused to allow the trial against Biggs to proceed and informed the jurors of his decision.

During the ninth week of the trial, the judge ordered that round-the-clock guards would be provided for the families of the 12 jurors while they were in retirement and the verdicts announced. On 28th March 1964, newspaper reports told of a man who was paid £10,000 by the gang to wipe all trace of them at the Leatherslade hideaway. The man got scared after the gang left and fled before he finished the job, leaving behind around 1,000 clues as to the gang's identity. As a result, it was believed that the man was living in terror for his life. Ten men had already been convicted in connection with the robbery and most of them faced several weeks in jail before knowing their sentences.

Boal, Wilson, Wisbey, Welch, Hussey, James and Goody were all found guilty of taking part and of conspiring to stop the Glasgow to London train before robbing it. Brian and Lennie Field were found not guilty of robbery but guilty of conspiring to stop the train and obstructing the course of justice, while Wheater was found guilty of conspiring to obstruct the course of justice.

Biggs went back on trial in April 1964 with a new jury, where he pleaded not guilty. He was eventually found guilty on 15th April and was sentenced alongside the 11 other men awaiting their fates. The hunt for Edwards, Reynolds and White continued even as the 12 men in the dock were sentenced to a total of 307 years between them. Biggs, Goody, Wilson, Wisbey, Welch, Hussey and James all received 30 years. Brian and Lennie Field were given 25 years, while Boal received 24. Cordrey got 20 years; Wheater was sentenced to three years. It was decided that Daly – whose prints were found only on the Monopoly board (and which could have happened at any point prior to the robbery) – had no case to answer to and he was acquitted. Alfred and Mary Pilgrim were cleared of receiving stolen money.

Having dealt with the sentencing, the judge went on to praise the men involved in bringing the criminals to justice, including the chief constable of Buckinghamshire, Brigadier John Cheney, Detective Superintendent Malcolm Fewtrell, Detective Sergeant Jack Pritchard from Scotland Yard and Detective Superintendent Gerald McArthur, also from the Yard. The police were confident that many from London's underworld would begin to talk. "Stolen money makes a lot of noise," said police. It was cited in newspapers at the time that Ethel Clark, from Bournemouth, John Ahern and Esa Hargrave who found the suitcases in Dorking, and the herdsman who uncovered the hideaway in Oakley, would all share in the reward money offered by the assessors.

On 11th May 1964, Jack Mills went back to work as a train driver, where he was welcomed by colleagues with handshakes and smiles. He was placed on light duties before finishing early on his first day due to his hard work. Two months later, the appeals of the men sentenced to 30 years in prison began. In July 1964 the Court of Criminal Appeal decided that the sentences would stand. All six appeals were dismissed by the court. However, both Brian Field and Lennie Field had their sentences cut to 14 years, while Boal's sentence was reduced by 10 years, as was Cordrey's. Then, in August 1964, Charles Wilson escaped from Winson Green Prison in Birmingham and a top-secret move to stop any more of the train robbery prisoners being "sprung" from jail was believed to be under way later that month. On 18th August, prison staff uncovered a plot to free Goody from Strangeways in Manchester; security at the prison was doubled and Goody himself was placed in solitary confinement.

At the end of May 1965, underworld sources informed police that Charlie Wilson had been killed by members of his own gang. The police didn't know whether or not to believe the stories, but they had found no trace of Wilson since he had escaped from prison and paid £40,000 to the gang who released him (Wilson was eventually caught in Canada in 1968 and returned to prison before being granted parole 10 years later.) Then, two months later in July 1965, Ronnie Biggs was "sprung" from jail leaving the Home Office and Britain's prison chiefs reeling. What Scotland Yard wanted to know was how it was allowed to happen and who was helping the plotters from inside Wandsworth Prison? The gang that helped to free Biggs and three other prisoners were known to have been armed, and police warned the public that the gang was dangerous. Biggs escaped overseas, first to Paris and later to Australia. Wilson was thought to be hiding out in Mexico City, if indeed he was still alive. James White was eventually captured, following a tip-off by a former friend, having been on the run for three years. He was arrested while at home with his wife Sheree and baby son. He had only £8,000 to give back to the police. His trial was held in June 1966, where he was sentenced to 18 years in prison.

Three months later, Buster Edwards was arrested at a house in Southwark Bridge Road, where he invited Detective Chief Superintendent Tom Butler, head of the Flying Squad, and his deputy Fred Williams, in for a cup of tea in the early hours of the morning. Edwards was charged at Aylesbury of conspiring to stop the train and with taking part in the robbery. In a statement, Edwards wrote: "For a long time now I have been going to give myself up. I was definitely going to come in, in a few weeks' time, but now I am glad I have made it now. I didn't do the train robbery like everybody said I did. That's why I have written this, because I want a fair deal. I didn't go up to the farm until after the robbery. My job was to clean it down and burn the rubbish. I did clean up some of it but something happened at the farm that night and I got the wind up. That was because the job was so big – I could hardly believe it. Some money was left in the kitchen for me. I was to get more after, but I never did. Although people think I got a lot, the truth is I didn't get very much. I have nothing left now, that's why I am giving myself up. The wife has been on to me to do it." Edwards was eventually jailed for 15 years for robbery and 12 years for conspiracy, with sentences to run concurrently – yet he was relieved that it was all over.

In January 1968, detectives were aiming to smash the gang after the capture of Wilson, who was traced to Montreal in Canada and flown back to the UK. Ronnie Biggs and Bruce Reynolds were next on the list, with the police confident that they would be caught. On 8th November 1968, Bruce Reynolds was at last in custody having been arrested in Torquay, Devon, by Detective Chief Superintendent Butler, who had been hunting for the criminal since 1963. At 6.15am, the Flying Squad and local "Q" cars moved in convoy towards Reynolds' home, a semi-detached house in one of the most exclusive areas of Torquay. Butler and his deputy rang the doorbell, which was answered by Reynolds' 6-year-old son dressed in his pyjamas. Six hours later, Reynolds arrived at Aylesbury police station and at 3.45pm was charged with conspiracy to stop and rob the mail train. He was eventually sentenced on 14th January 1969 to 25 years for his leading role in the robbery. During his five years on the run, he used forged passports that took him halfway around the world, where he lived in luxury apartments, wore the best clothes and drove expensive cars. His arrest brought an end to a life of crime that had started 20 years previously with an assault on a policeman. Reynolds had ended up in borstal before serving subsequent sentences for burglaries and receiving stolen goods, wounding with intent and another assault on police. He was released from jail in June 1978 after serving 10 years.

Douglas Goody went on to live a relatively successful life on his release from prison, later living in Majorca. Charlie Wilson was shot dead in Marbella in 1990 as a result of suspected drug-dealing activities. Buster Edwards, despite a successful business as a flower-stall holder in London, committed suicide in 1994. Ronnie Biggs eventually moved to Brazil in order to escape the authorities, which were closing the net around his home in Australia. There were no extradition arrangements in place between Brazil and Britain and he lived a good life in Rio de Janeiro with his family untouched by British authority, despite the fact that the British police had arrested him in Rio in February 1974. He was freed in a stunning decision by the Brazilian Government in May that same year. He returned to the UK voluntarily in 2001 after suffering from a number of strokes. By now, Biggs was 71 years old and had spent more than 35 years on the run. But Biggs wanted to give himself up, even though many in the UK thought that he should stay away. The birth of Biggs' son Michael by his Brazilian girlfriend Raimunda had given him immunity in the country he adopted as home. Many in Britain, including Norman Brennan, director of the Victims of Crime Trust, were confident that the UK should have nothing more to do with the former criminal. One of those willing to come forward to talk about Biggs was John Mills, the son of train driver Jack Mills, who had watched his father suffer since he was injured in the robbery. Mills senior had only lived for a further six years after the raid and had suffered from headaches ever since. He died of leukaemia at the age of 64 but John Mills firmly believed that the beating his father had taken had also contributed to his life being cut short. Even the Home Office stated that if Biggs thought he'd gain any sympathy in the UK he would be in for a shock.

It might have been the biggest heist in Britain's history at that time, but many of the robbers lost their money or had it stolen by unreliable "minders", or they spent it trying to escape the authorities or paying legal fees. In truth, what should have provided some of the best criminal masterminds in the country with a comfortable lifestyle offering only the best, actually destroyed more lives than it improved. Innocent victims such as Jack Mills, the post office staff and Dave Whitby, who was just 26 years old at the time of the robbery, were severely affected and left with a sad, enduring and pointless legacy.

Linwood Bank Robbery

(1969)

Howard Wilson was a man on a mission. He'd resigned from the police force in Scotland when he became disillusioned with his lot in life. Wilson had failed to make significant promotions during his 10 years on the force, and subsequently found his two greengrocery businesses suffering from serious debt problems. He needed a way out and he thought he had the answer. On 30th December 1969, Howard Wilson led a small gang of men, including John Sim – an ex-policeman turned salesman – and car mechanic Ian Donaldson to the Bridge Street branch of the Clydesdale Bank in Linwood near Glasgow to commit a robbery.

It probably wasn't the first time the gang had committed a bank robbery; it was widely accepted that they had attacked the British Linen Bank in Williamwood, Glasgow, some months previously. The three men were suspected to have carried out the raid with the help of a fourth man, unnamed, who was later rumoured to have been buried in the pillars of the Kingston Bridge (opened in 1970), which may be somewhat dubious although the fourth man has never been traced. Wilson was the leading man and brainchild of the robberies. Tall and smartly dressed, he was a particularly bitter man, yet deluded about what he was capable of doing. His two greengrocer shops were rapidly losing money and he was, in spite of his faith in himself, a broken man – on the edge and extremely desperate. The two men he chose to help him in his quest were equally as down on their luck: the bank job seemed to be the perfect "get-out" card. Wilson, Sim and Donaldson legally bought a Russian Vostok .22 from the president of the Bearsden Shooting Club where all three were members, thus nothing seemed untoward or out of the ordinary. To complete the complement of gang members, Archibald McGeachie was recruited as the getaway driver.

In July 1969, the gang descended on the British Linen Bank in Williamwood, where they pulled off a heist involving more than £20,000. Dressed as businessmen, the staff at the bank hadn't suspected the three men until a gun was pulled and ammonia was squirted in the eyes of the cashiers. At this point, the death penalty in Scotland still existed. As the gang remained "low" and didn't "splash the cash", no one suspected the four men of their involvement in the raid. The proceeds were split and life went back to normal for a short time, until all three of the main gang members found themselves suffering mounting business debts and it became a necessity to repeat the crime. The young getaway driver, McGeachie, for reasons unknown declined to take part in the second bank raid planned on the Clydesdale Bank. He left his home on 23rd December 1969 and was never seen or heard of again. Just a few weeks earlier, the death penalty in Scotland had been abolished.

One theory offered is that the gang viewed him as a weak link, and perhaps a risk that needed to be silenced on a permanent basis. Was McGeachie's body really dumped in one of the concrete stanchions supporting the Kingston Bridge that was under construction at the time? Strong rumours surrounded the disappearance of the young man, but nothing was ever proved at the time, or when the bridge was refurbished in the 1990s due to the increase in traffic that it had to cope with. However, it was widely suspected that Howard Wilson, bright and articulate, was capable of killing a man, dumping his body and getting away with it.

Following the raid at the Clydesdale Bank, Wilson and his gang made for his flat at 51 Allison Street, Goyanhill. The haul amounted to just over £14,000, which the men had stashed in suitcases. In addition to the cash, the gang had also stolen a large metal box full of coins. As the men began unloading the car at Wilson's flat, there was nothing really going on that would alert a passer-by to the situation. However, what they didn't realize was that they were being watched by a policeman who had never liked or trusted his former colleague. Inspector Andrew Hyslop happened to be in a shop across the street from Wilson's flat and witnessed the men unloading the vehicle. He was intrigued and decided to investigate further by taking a closer look. Unaware that Wilson and his cronies had just committed a robbery, Inspector Hyslop moved forward, where he was greeted by Wilson in a jovial and friendly manner. Wilson invited his former colleague in for a drink.

Hyslop had already radioed and asked fellow police officers to meet him at the flat as back-up, so he wasn't too concerned when Wilson gave him permission to look in one of the suitcases. As he did so, and saw the bank notes, Wilson pulled a gun and pointed it at Hyslop's face. Wilson pulled the trigger but the gun jammed. He tried again and shot Andrew Hyslop in the face. The bullet reached the inspector's skull at about the same time as three policemen arrived on the scene and entered the room. Wilson was a trained marksman and shot both Detective Constable Angus MacKenzie and Constable Edward Barnett in the head. Constable John Sellars managed to escape the room and radio for help while finding refuge in the bathroom. Seeing that Angus MacKenzie was still alive, Wilson walked over to the injured police officer, pointed his gun at the constable's forehead and fired. Angus MacKenzie was shot dead.

Wilson was about to kill Inspector Andrew Hyslop with his one remaining bullet when he was intercepted by the arrival and quick thinking of Constable John Campbell, who immediately dived on the killer as he entered the room. The gun went off during the struggle and the bullet lodged itself in the ceiling. The situation was over. Inspector Hyslop was alive, but suffered from bullet fragments in his skull and was confined to a wheelchair for the remainder of his life. He had to retire from the police force as a result of his injuries and never fully recovered from the fact that two of his esteemed colleagues had been shot dead. Constable Barnett died within a few days of the shooting.

Each member of the gang was found guilty of robbery and sentenced to 12 years. Both Sim and Donaldson had had nothing to do with the shootings or murder; Donaldson had, in fact, fled the scene at the start of the trauma. Wilson pleaded guilty to two murders at Edinburgh High Court in February 1970 and was sentenced to life imprisonment. After the sentencing, a large group of women from policemen's families from all over Scotland descended on George

Square demonstrating for the return of the death penalty abolished just a short time before. They were desperate for Wilson to hang for his crimes and almost succeeded in persuading Scottish officials that he should. Wilson, for his part, was a difficult prisoner and caused and participated in a number of riots and attacks before he began finally to settle down in jail.

Andrew Hyslop and John Campbell were both awarded the George Medal for their bravery during the attack, while Angus MacKenzie and Edward Barnett were posthumously awarded the Queen's Police Medal.

After serving almost 33 years in prison, Wilson was released on parole at the age of 64 in September 2002. After settling down in prison, the former policeman and two-time killer wrote a number of crime novels, including *Angels of Death*, a bestseller that received the Koestler Award.

Lloyds, Baker Street, London

(1971)

A big question mark hung over the police handling of the London Walkie-Talkie Bank Raid on Lloyds Bank at the junction of Baker Street and Marylebone Road on 13th September 1971. Scotland Yard tried to find out just how the bandits beat the tremendous odds stacked against them to escape with a huge haul. Yard investigators wanted to know the answer to a number of disturbing questions arising from the grab of money and jewels from the branch. The raiders had dodged the bank's security system by tunnelling into the vault from a shop two doors away, where – using walkie-talkie radios to keep in touch with a lookout man posted at the top of a block of flats – they had managed to foil London's police. Officers had been tipped off about the robbery by a radio amateur who picked up the walkie-talkie signals.

The gang, which included a woman, had a huge stroke of luck as the police set about checking 700 London banks following the alert. The gang were cracking safe-deposit boxes in the vault when Lloyds security inspectors and police officers arrived on the scene. The raiders kept quiet and sat tight as bank staff and police determined that alarms were in order and the vault doors had not been tampered with. The investigating team, assuming that all was in order, left the bank and the raiders continued opening safe-deposit boxes, some of which contained valuables worth up to £500,000. The gang had burst through the floor with a thermic lance and then escaped with their haul on the Sunday afternoon.

Scotland Yard wanted to know why the post office detector service was not called until midday on the Sunday, when it was too late for them to do anything. The gang had toiled for 13 hours tunnelling into the bank's vault and, for the majority of that time, the police were listening in to the two-way radio conversation between the raiders and their lookout man. Radio amateur Robert Rowlands, 32, picked up the gang's signals over the radio at around 11.30pm, just as he was going to bed at his flat in Wimpole Street about half a mile away from the bank. He began recording the conversations he was hearing when he heard one of the men say: "We're sitting on £500,000." He then alerted police. One of the voices he recorded was believed to be that of a gang member posted on the top of a block of flats with a pair of binoculars. Police believed he was stationed there to watch for anyone who might be showing a dangerous interest in the bank. Some of the conversation follows:

First raider: "Listen carefully. We want you to mind for one hour from now until approximately one o'clock and then to go off the air, get some sleep and come on the air with both radios at six o'clock in the morning."

Second raider: "This is not a very good pitch during the day. You know that don't you? It's all blowing about and everything."

First raider: "Are you sure you will be on the street tomorrow? I suggest we carry on tonight mate and get it done with." The raider continued: "Look, the place is filled with fumes where we was cutting.

And if the security come in and smell the fumes we are all going to get stopped and none of us have got nothing. This way, we have all got 300 grand to cut up when we come back in the morning."

The man on the roof did not appear to be very happy with the arrangement and told his fellow gang member that he wasn't going to be any good the following day. He was advised by the first raider to get some sleep. However, the pleading from the roof continued. The night did seem to pass uneventfully for the lookout, who reported in the morning that everything was fine.

Post office engineers had failed to get an accurate fix on the locations of the walkie-talkies and the police search had ended in failure. During the hunt for the robbers, the police had checked on the bank but, like security staff, could find nothing amiss. Their crucial mistake, however, was not opening the doors to the vault. The raid was discovered on Monday, 13th September by bank manager Guy Darke, long after the gang had gone. It was then determined that the gang had tunnelled more than 40ft through sand and earth from the handbag shop two doors away, before they reached the 4ft thick reinforced concrete floor of the bank vault. The gang had left behind their tools, including the radio set, hammers, picks, shovels, gas cylinders and thermic lances (a favourite tool amongst thieves for cutting concrete or metal within seconds). Police also found half-eaten food and flasks at the raid site; most of the basement of the neighbouring shop was full of earth that had come from the tunnel.

Security guards at Lloyds were stunned by the news that an "impregnable" vault had been broken into. A Lloyds spokesman said:

"Our security people who went with the police to the bank were satisfied that everything was working properly on Sunday, and that nothing had been tampered with. Our security system is comprehensive and very complicated. It appeared to the inspection team that there was absolutely nothing wrong."

Police were puzzled by the small size of the hole through which the raiders got into the vault. It was only 15in wide, so police suspected that a small woman, or a child, may have been involved; one of the voices picked up on the radio was a woman. Senior detectives agreed that the job was brilliantly professional but wondered if the gang had been disturbed as only one-quarter of the safe-deposit boxes were robbed. Guy Darke was also stunned by the news that his bank had been raided. Returning from a holiday, he was overwhelmed with safe-deposit-box holders demanding news of their valuables, despite the fact that the bank was closed for business on the Monday following the robbery. "One couple, told that their valuables worth £5,000 were safe, kept hugging each other with tears pouring down their faces," said the bank manager.

Just two days after the robbery, an inquiry into the way the police had handled the bank raid was started by Scotland Yard. The investigating team had been told to find out whether or not the police were negligent as the thieves tunnelled their way into the vault. Despite the fact that police had been listening in to the live walkie-talkie conversations, they failed to ask engineers to trace the source of the radios until more than 12 hours after the raid began. By then, it was too late and the signals had stopped transmitting. The case became more mysterious when former washing machine tycoon John Bloom denied having a safe-deposit box at the bank with valuables worth up to £100,000. It was reportedly one of the 215 smashed boxes robbed during the raid, but Bloom was adamant that the box wasn't his. His wife confirmed that the couple had used the branch in 1966 but stated categorically that they had never had an account at the bank. However, someone called John Bloom did lose around £70,000 worth of gems and £30,000 of cash in the raid. The most valuable loss was thought to be a sheaf of confidential papers containing the names of business people and details of planned business ventures. These also contained details of plans to sell colour TVs for £72.

Meanwhile, in the hunt for the gang, the police were concentrating their efforts on a country mansion thought to be the home of a man who plotted and financed the robbery. By the end of the month during which the raid took place, the value of the booty was estimated to be around £4 million as detectives slowly traced the owners of 50 of the total 215 safe-deposit boxes that were smashed open. The estimated total made the robbery the largest ever heist in Britain at the time – bigger than the Great Train Robbery some eight years before with a total of £2.6 million – even though very little of the haul appeared to be in cash. For the most part, it was gold, diamonds and other gems that the robbers managed to seize. By 24th September, detectives had the names of two men that they wanted to interview, both of whom were well known in London circles; both had also disappeared from their usual haunts. One was said to be a dead-ringer for the film star Kirk Douglas, with a prominent cleft chin, while police were also hunting for a mysterious woman who had been spotted on several occasions shopping in the area prior to the robbery. A number of witnesses had described the woman, who wore a variety of wigs.

By January 1973 the police had already found three of the raiders, who admitted entering the bank, stealing cash and valuables and possessing explosives. Thomas Stephens, 35, from Islington, 37-year-old Reginald Tucker of Lee Street, Hackney and 38-year-old Anthony Gavin from Dalston were on trial at the Old Bailey. However, Benjamin Wolfe, 64, from East Dulwich denied charges; and Abdullah Gangji, 62, and his nephew Ackbar Gangji, 22, denied receiving £32,000 in stolen notes and helping to dispose of the money. The raid, which played out like a Sir Arthur Conan Doyle *Sherlock Holmes* mystery – and took place just around the corner from Holmes' fictional address on Baker Street – was dubbed "The Baker Street Moles".

By now, the final amount stolen had been confirmed at £3 million and it had proved to be Britain's biggest robbery to date. Despite the fact that four men were in custody over the raid, only £231,000 had been recovered. Facing the jury at the Old Bailey was Tucker, convicted and sentenced to 12 years for his part in the robbery. The former funfair attendant, newsagent and car dealer had been recruited as the gang's reconnaissance man. He had opened a safe-deposit account at the bank (although he had little to deposit) so that he could gain access to the vaults and make copies of their layout (while alone in the vaults, Tucker showed ingenuity by measuring the room using his umbrella). His share of the loot had been left in a luggage locker at Waterloo Station. Stephens, a car dealer, was also jailed for 12 years.

He had provided the tools for digging the tunnel and had helped by removing 15 tons of rubble. The man who planned and constructed the tunnel was Anthony Gavin, who also received a 12-year sentence. Gavin had lost 1.5st while carrying out the preliminary digging towards the bank vault from the neighbouring handbag shop. His loot was left in a locker at Euston Station. Benjamin Wolfe was jailed for eight years for his part in the heist, given a shorter sentence as the judge, Edward Sutcliffe, QC, did not want the older man to spend the rest of his life in prison. The leather shop two doors from the bank had been taken over by Wolfe, who denied that he knew anything about the gang breaking into the bank. However, police officials and court authorities were mindful that the mastermind behind the robbery was nowhere near the court and was not standing trial alongside the "gang". Derek Larkins was wanted by police for questioning as was a man known as Ginger John (mentioned during questioning by Gavin), however, there was no evidence to prove their involvement.

At a special press conference given by Scotland Yard, CID Commander Robert Huntley defended the way that the bank robbery was investigated, saying that three west London police divisions were alerted to the raid, but had no way of pinpointing the bank inside a wide radius. Radio amateur Rowlands had picked up the sound of roadworks and other clues, but there were six other banks and four other buildings holding large amounts of cash in the area that could have been involved. Commander Huntley revealed that detectives twice asked the Post Office for detector vans to track down the bandits' radios, but no help was forthcoming. He also pointed out that the press had been asked not to print the contents of the conversations picked up by Rowlands, yet they had – and he claimed this had led to a lengthened police investigation. In addition, the police were prohibited for quite some time by Lloyds Bank of knowing exactly who the victims of the crime were and exactly what had been taken. The bank raid was almost a carbon copy of one of the most famous robberies in fiction entitled *The Red-Headed League*, a short story by Sir Arthur Conan Doyle with Sherlock Holmes as the sleuth who tracked down the robbers. The book, written in 1890, follows the story of a group of criminals who take over a pawnbroker's shop adjoining a London bank prior to attempting a robbery. The thieves patiently tunnelled for days between shop and bank before being caught by the great detective. In the real robbery, it took Scotland Yard slightly longer than the fictional detective to bring the perpetrators to justice.

In 1977, the High Court in London was told by Raymond Kidwell, QC, that the security at Lloyds Bank was "wholly inefficient" and that the bank had been negligent both before and after the 1971 raid. Before the raid, gang member Tucker had cased the joint on no less than 14 occasions while, after the raid, the bank was less than vigilant when allowing people in to take their valuables left piled on tables. In some cases, people weren't even checked to see if they actually were depositors. Kidwell argued in court that: "The system would have facilitated and doubtless did facilitate, people getting valuables which were not theirs. Property went widely and wildly astray." The QC was representing 139 people claiming £666,000 in valuables stolen in the robbery. The bank claimed that it was not responsible for the losses unless negligence could be proved.

Bank of America Robbery

(1975)

When news was announced of the Bank of America robbery in April 1975, it was estimated that bandits had got away with a staggering £2 million. And, it looked as if it wasn't the gang's first attempt at an American bank. In November 1974, robbers had been foiled because their drills were too short to penetrate the massive vault door fully. Dubbed the Mayfair Mob, the robbers made no such mistake when four armed raiders drilled their way into the vault at the Davies Street branch of Bank of America. They used a jemmy to force open 89 safe-deposit boxes and got away with £250,000 in cash – they ignored £1 million in travellers' cheques, which would have been hard to get rid off – and an extremely valuable haul of gems and other valuables.

One customer, Farida Hall, 38, put her uninsured loss at £200,000. She had lost her entire jewellery collection, including nine rings, two diamond brooches, two diamond pendants and five pairs of jewelled earrings. Mrs Hall, the daughter of a sugar exporter, had kept her jewellery in the bank for eight years and had never insured it as she believed it to be safe within the bank. Police and bank officials contacted all key holders whose boxes were rifled, but the major "headache" for the investigation was to establish what had been taken from the confidential boxes. One depositor, American businessman John Pugliese, had six gold coins worth up to six figures in his safe-deposit box. However, he was insured. One particularly worried customer was 23-year-old student John Phillips, from Bloomsbury in London, who had a number of gold coins worth several thousand pounds.

The raid was discovered by a patrolling security guard who reached the bank at 8.38pm and found three staff – two men and a woman – bound and gagged. The three victims had been working late in an upstairs office when they were caught by the gang. One of the gang had hid inside the bank until it closed in order to let other members inside – this was the same method of entry used by the gang in November the previous year. At the time, the California-based Bank of America was the world's largest bank and the robbery was cited as one of the biggest hauls in recent years. The man hiding inside the bank knocked out the alarm system and kicked in the door to an underground passage in Three Kings Yard before unlocking the door and allowing his fellow accomplices into the premises. The plan – despite the three late workers – went like clockwork and in the words of one senior detective was the work of "a good team of professional thieves".

The gang had detailed knowledge of the bank's layout and the alarms were shut down easily and quickly. After the gang tied up the members of staff in the basement, they then continued to work their way into the vault using drills. All four gang members were armed, and seemed to have had information about the structure of the combination lock on the steel vault door. Using an ordinary power drill, they bored through points on the lock near the combination numbers. Once inside, the raiders loaded their haul into bags and left the bank through the underground passage. Just eight minutes later – and two hours after the robbery began – security guard Bob Gordon discovered the crime while on his rounds.

Police investigations led them to 32-year-old James O'Loughlin, who was tried at London's Marlborough Street Magistrates Court on 28th July 1975. He was accused of conspiracy in the raid, and police watched in puzzlement as O'Loughlin made bail. The police just couldn't believe that the man from Gate Road, Kingston in Surrey, could get bail. As he walked calmly past them and left the court, it became clear, however, that O'Loughlin (who stood charged alongside five other men) had asked to go to the toilet in order to calmly make his escape. The men had been remanded in custody until August, and had left the dock to make their way to the cells below to await a prison van. O'Loughlin was believed to have left the toilet and walked past other prisoners to trick court police into thinking that he had been granted bail. A hurried search around the court after the alarm was raised confirmed that he had managed to make a clear break.

At the end of September 1975, electronics expert Stuart Buckley was jailed for seven years at the Old Bailey when the court heard how he had used an ingenious method to find the combination of the bank safe. Working as an electrical contractor at the bank, he had watched through a spy-hole in a false ceiling as the manager operated the dial. He then tipped off the gang on when to rob the bank. Buckley admitted to stealing £2.25 million from the Bank of America but became a marked man for naming the rest of the gang. Buckley had been given a job with the bank as an electrician just nine months after being released from prison; Bank of America was unaware he was a crook and he soon became trusted by other staff members. He was given access to all the bank's branches in London and was able to gain most of the keys to all areas.

By March 1976, police believed that the gang had actually got away with £8 million when owners of 85 of the safe-deposit boxes revealed how much they had lost in cash and valuables. By this time, there were 17 people awaiting trial in connection with the crime. On 11th June that same year, company director John O'Connell, 41, was gunned down as he made his way from his home to a bus stop nearby while en route to face trial. The hit man was hiding behind a bush in a church yard and was believed to have escaped in a car, probably driven by an accomplice, after he blasted O'Connell with a shotgun. O'Connell had been hit in the leg and was rushed to hospital from Church Vale in East Finchley, north London, for an emergency operation. He had been due to appear at the Old Bailey alongside seven other men and a woman. Key witnesses in the case had already been given armed bodyguards. However, following the attack on O'Connell, the judge, Alan King-Hamilton, said that jury members would be given a police escort to and from the court.

In November 1976 three men were found guilty of the robbery, including Leonard Wilde, 51, Peter Colson, 32, and William Gear, 44. Wilde's wife, Vivienne, 41, was found not guilty of receiving. Later in November, five men received jail sentences for a total of more than 100 years. Wilde, an underworld locksmith, was given the longest sentence at 23 years. He was also sentenced to 12 years for the earlier plot to rob the bank in November 1974, which was to run concurrently.

Colson was jailed for 21 years; Gear got 18 years; O'Loughlin, who had been recaptured, got 17 years; and the fifth man, 52-year-old Henry Jeffery, received 12 years. Henry Taylor, a greengrocer who let the robbers use his shop to share out the loot, was given three years. Croupier Edward Gerty, 34, received two years for receiving stolen money and jewellery; and Michael Gervaise, 33, who was found guilty of taking part in the first unsuccessful plan, was jailed for 18 months. Buckley, as the star prosecution witness, was said to be in fear of his life. The missing treasure, however, had not been found.

The man the papers called "Mr Big", ringleader Frank Maple, 37, had escaped to his villa in Marbella, Spain, after the first raid in 1974. Following a big round-up by Scotland Yard, he was arrested and then released because extradition papers did not arrive from London in time. Maple then fled to Morocco, which had no extradition treaty with Britain. He was known to have been involved in other London heists, including defrauding Christie's and Sotheby's auction rooms. Maple's mistake was to enter Greece, where he was arrested in June 1977 – and police believed he would be extradited to the UK. However, the former gang leader was also wanted in Austria in connection with the theft of £120,000 in cash and jewellery in an armed raid at a ski resort in February that year. As the tug of war for custody of Maple raged on, Scotland Yard announced that they also wanted 35-year-old David Carroll, known as Boy-Boy, who vanished after the Mayfair raid. Eventually, in September 1977, Austria won the fight to extradite Maple. Meanwhile, O'Connell, who had been crippled by the unknown hit man, hobbled to freedom from the Old Bailey in December, having been given a two-year suspended sentence 12 months after other members of the gang were jailed.

Frank Maple was jailed for nine years in April 1978 for the robbery of a hotel at an Austrian ski resort. He was due to be extradited to the UK once he had served one-third of his sentence. The following year, Vivienne Wilde went into hiding after claiming that a high-ranking police officer had been paid more than £7,000 for acting as "Mr Fix-it" for the gang. Police feared that a contract had been put out on Mrs Wilde's life for "grassing" on the officer and for claiming that he was paid money for the deals he made with criminals to protect them from prosecution. The police mounted "Operation Countryman" to look into the allegations, part of an ongoing investigation during which five officers had already been suspended. Then, on 5th November 1982, Frank Maple walked free from the Old Bailey after the prosecution offered no evidence against him.

Peter Colson served his sentence for the Bank of America robbery but, unfortunately, didn't learn that crime doesn't pay. Just one year after his release he was caught trying to rob a security van in November 1987 while posing as a dispatch rider. He received a new sentence of 16 years.

British Bank of the Middle East

(1976)

It has been widely accepted that a splinter group of the Palestine Liberation Organization (PLO) took advantage of Lebanon's state of chaos caused by civil war and, using brute force, smashed its way into the British Bank of the Middle East (BBME) in Beirut on 20th January 1976, where the raid carried out saw the robbers make off with an estimated £25m – worth about £100m at today's prices.

Today, the PLO is recognized as the sole representative of the Palestinian people by the United Nations and across 100 states with which the group holds diplomatic relations. The group was considered to be a terrorist one until the Madrid Conference of 1991. Two years later, the PLO agreed and recognized Israel's right to exist in peace and accepted UN Security Council resolutions, while rejecting violence and terrorism. In return, Israel officially recognized the PLO as the representative of the Palestinian people. However, in 1976 things were less clear cut and extremely volatile.

During the raid, bandits blasted through a wall that the bank shared with a Catholic church, cracked the bank's vaults and took its loot in gold bars along with stocks, foreign currency (FX), jewels and Lebanese currency. Today, the treasure is still missing, those responsible have never been brought to justice and the robbers haven't even been found. It was, at the time, the largest bank heist ever known.

A small, elite group of men took part in the raid. Each was heavily armed with state-of-the-art equipment; every man was meant to be unrecognizable and to remain unrecognizable during their assault on the Bab-Idriss branch of the BBME. The bank itself was one of the most eminent and oldest banks in Lebanon at the time and, despite the damage caused to the building by the continuing civil war, still proudly displayed its logo (which, due to firing in the area, had seen better days). The bank, which lay at the centre of the country's financial district, found itself in no-man's land with Christians to the east and Muslims in the west. Despite warring factions, the bank was still operating as normally as it could in a building that surrounded its impregnable vault. But, there were those who were well aware of the fortune sitting inside the vault and, as far as the robbers were concerned, it was there for the taking.

Having smashed their way into the bank, the gang needed to access the vault, which they did by blasting through a wall. The largest heist in banking history had just been carried out but, despite the magnitude of the haul, the case remained little publicized in the world press. It remains the biggest ever bank robbery in the world and, despite its lack of coverage, there are those fascinated by the story and how the robbers got away with such an epic haul. Once the robbery was made public, warring factions blamed each other for the heist, but no one really knows whether the PLO were responsible for the crime or not. There was much speculation, and still is today, about who was responsible and why. What does seem strange, however, is that for a robbery of such magnitude, why is the story so little known?

After all, Lebanon was at the centre of world terrorism at the time, so how come no one seems to know anything? All other major robberies seem to hit the headlines within minutes of happening, and much is known about details on the ground quite early on – even those the authorities would rather were not known. Perhaps it is possible that the PLO were not involved but that another, different type of organization was responsible. Either way, nothing is confirmed and no one is saying publicly what really happened.

Security Express

(1983)

Armed raiders escaped with up to £7 million on 4th April 1983 in one of Britain's biggest ever cash robberies. The money had been collected by Security Express vans from factories, banks and supermarkets throughout London during the Easter holiday and stored in a vault at the firm's headquarters in Curtain Road, Shoreditch ready for banking on 5th April. The gang, who were hooded, were waiting inside the building when seven cashiers and guards turned up for work. One by one, the staff were overpowered and forced at gunpoint to hand over keys and give details of the vault security system. Each was then bound and gagged and the gang – consisting of at least six members – then cleaned out the huge store of notes and coins.

It was two and a half hours after the raiders left before the staff managed to free themselves and raise the alarm. The crooks got into the building during the night by climbing over a back wall and managed to avoid floodlights and closed-circuit TV. They were able to take their time because the surrounding streets, offices and shops were deserted for the holiday weekend. At 7.00am they surprised the guard on the door and forced their way inside. They then waited for five hours for other staff to arrive.

Commander Frank Cater, head of Scotland Yard's Flying Squad, together with the Central Robbery Squad, led a team of 40 detectives in the investigation. City of London detectives based at City Road police station questioned the Security Express staff in an effort to get descriptions of the raiders. Meanwhile, forensic experts examined the alarm system in the four-storey building. One major puzzle that faced the police was how the gang managed to drive off with such a bulky load of cash. They were believed to have spent two hours removing it from the vault, and at least two vehicles would have been needed to cart away the haul. The raid came when the building, which was permanently guarded, was at its most vulnerable because of the bank holiday, yet the vault contained record takings. During the police investigation, it transpired that a raider threatened to burn one of the guards alive unless the vault was opened. The guard was told he would be doused in petrol and set alight if he and other staff did not co-operate with the gang.

On 5th April, a reward of £500,000 was offered – the largest ever offered in the UK – by Lloyds underwriters for the capture of the gang and the recovery of the cash. It was hoped that the reward – which was offered tax-free – would tempt underworld "supergrasses" into coming forward. The gang, carrying shotguns and wearing hoods or masks, struck after seizing seven hostages. The staff at Security Express, fearing for their lives, reluctantly obeyed the raiders. A manager, who remained unnamed, told police that: "Staff don't argue. They have instructions not to resist and risk their lives. It's the only chink in our armour." De La Rue, the parent company of Security Express, confirmed that the haul was in the region of £7 million. A spokesman for the company said: "We reckon the gang would have needed at least two large vans to transport that amount away."

The hostages were questioned for several days following the robbery, as police began visiting the homes of known and suspected criminals. Gangland figures were also approached in London and the Home Counties. Senior officers were convinced that a "mole" in the company helped mastermind the plan by giving the gang inside information. Police believed that the elaborate operation, which took eight hours, could not have been carried out without specialized knowledge of the depot's layout and security systems. On 6th April, 19-year-old Noel McHenry went into hiding, fearing for his life after he gave the police vital information about the robbery. He told detectives how he had been working at a printing plant near the Security Express headquarters and that, when he left to go home, he noticed strange cars in the street; the road would normally have been deserted over the bank holiday. He also stated that he got quite a good look at a number of men hanging around near the cars. After being grilled by police about what exactly he had witnessed, the terrified teenager was advised to keep low for a few days. He was warned not to talk to anyone or to go back to work. He took some holiday from the printers where he worked and left his home in Bethnal Green, London, where he lived with his parents. Scotland Yard then made a fresh appeal for information when they were surprised that no one from the underworld had come forward, given the large reward on offer.

A breakthrough came the following week. Officers holidaying in southern Spain noticed that a large amount of money was being spent in seaside resorts and three detectives were sent out to Spain. In May, it was reported that more than £6 million would be paid out in insurance claims to those firms that had lost their money. Settlements were speeded up to prevent hardship to 50 large and small businesses who had cash stolen. Several major banks and supermarket companies, along with high street shops, the London Electricity Board and North Thames Gas were believed to have lost more than £1 million between them.

Then, in January 1984, three men were charged with being involved in the raid, including William Hickson, 40, Terence Perkins, 35, and John Horsley, 41. At the beginning of 1985, two former brothers-in-law of the actress Barbara Windsor were accused of being involved. Garage owner John Knight, 48, denied helping to plan the heist, while his brother James, 59, denied handling the proceeds of the raid. They appeared in the dock at the Old Bailey alongside four other men. Both Knight brothers were convicted for their parts in the crime and, in June 1985, their brother, Ronnie Knight, vowed to return to Britain to clear his name. Speaking from his villa on the Costa del Sol in Spain, Knight told reporters: "I'm just choked about my brothers." He was one of five men that police still wanted to question in connection with the crime.

At the same time, a "mole" who was believed to have been working for Security Express for up to 15 years at the time of the robbery was identified as having given the gang inside information. He was being hunted by police for his part in the well-planned operation. The police had struggled for a number of months following the robbery to glean any significant information, until an underworld tip-off led them to the Knight brothers, Terence Perkins and William Hickson. John Horsley had already admitted to the robbery. Accountant Robert Young was cleared of handling stolen money, as was Perkins' wife, Jacqueline. Another member of the gang, 36-year-old Allen Opiola had turned informer as the net closed and, after receiving a prison sentence the year before, had moved to the south of England where he was living under an assumed name. While working for John Knight, his involvement had meant getting hold of four vehicles and four large suitcases to be used in the raid. Opiola and his wife had one-third of the haul brought to their house, where they were responsible for counting the money.

Laundering the money proved a huge headache for the gang. Small amounts were paid into building society and bank accounts, and bundles of notes were taken out of the country in hand luggage. The gang was then known to have gone on spending sprees in Britain, Spain and Portugal. Gang members bought villas and flats, and it took the police months to trace the Spanish connection. In June 1985, the raiders were jailed for a total of 66 years. Ringleaders John Knight and Terence Perkins each got 22 years. John Horsley got eight years for his confession (which helped to put others behind bars) and James Knight got eight years for handling the cash. Hickson was also found guilty of handling and was given a six-year sentence. There was evidence that the ringleaders had stowed away large sums in Spain and Guernsey but, at this stage, only £2 million had been traced.

By February 1989, the Spanish were set to clear up the "Costa del Crime" as it had become known. The authorities planned to get tough in an attempt to rid themselves of undesirables and Britain's criminal classes, who were renowned for escaping to the area. Some of the most famous fugitives from British justice were about to be booted out of their luxury hideaways by expulsion orders signed by a top Madrid judge, in a secret session as part of the new get-tough policy.

Nine fugitives were known to be under threat, including Ronnie Knight – who refused to return to Britain unless the authorities gave him four weeks without being arrested; Freddie Foreman (the bully boy enforcer for the Kray gang), Clifford Saxe, Ronnie Everett, John Mason, Keith Cottingham (wanted for murder), James Jeffrey, John Corscadden and Michael Green. Clifford Saxe, 63, confirmed to newspapers that for him: "The game was up." Saxe, a former Hackney publican and East End villain, said he was too old to run. He fully expected to be apprehended by the police on his return to Britain.

Ronnie Knight eventually agreed that his time on the Costa del Crime was probably over and vowed that he would fight to clear his name if he returned home. In April 1990, Freddie Foreman, known as the godfather of the Costa del Crime, was finally convicted for his part in the Security Express crime. He was cleared of taking part in the robbery but found guilty of dishonestly handling more than £350,000 of the haul. It was believed he used the money to set up a drugs empire from his refuge in Spain. He was jailed for nine years following Spain's decision to boot him out. The former "heavy" for the Kray gang was arrested as he arrived in London in 1989.

In a dramatic twist in October 1990, Ronnie Knight won his case to stay in Spain when a Spanish judge turned down Scotland Yard's attempts to extradite him. But Knight returned to the UK in 1994, where he was arrested at Luton airport in connection with the Security

Express robbery. After 11 years as a fugitive in Spain, and despite protestations from Knight of his innocence, he was locked up. It transpired that Knight had been faced with a grim choice in Spain and preferred to fly home and face a seven-year jail sentence. It was Knight's involvement with London's modern-day crooks that ended his life on the run (with his wife Sue Haylock), as just two weeks before he flew back to Britain he had been confronted by a gunman who put a pistol to Knight's head and pulled the trigger. The gun was empty and Knight fell to the floor pleading for his life. Through clenched teeth, the gunman told him: "Next time, Ronnie", and walked away. Ronnie could stay and face certain death, or he could choose the British justice system and jail. He chose the latter.

Police believe that the haul was divided into shares of £400,000 and £500,000 within 48 hours of the raid and that accountant Albert Fox was duped into "laundering" the money. Believing the money to be legitimate proceeds of property deals, Fox distributed the cash around Europe in various bank accounts. He later helped the police retrace the money trail to show where the money was hidden in Jersey, Guernsey, Gibraltar and Spain.

Brinks Mat Bullion Raid

(1983)

Following a £25 million gold haul from a Heathrow Airport warehouse in November 1983, security experts claimed that huge stocks of gold bullion at depots throughout the country were sitting targets for raiders. Depots in Birmingham, Bristol, Leeds and Warrington were all vulnerable to attack from gangs such as the one that beat the high-security premises of Brinks Mat. Detectives refused to disclose how the six raiders got in and out of the warehouse on the trading estate complex just outside the airport's security area, but it was believed that they lay in wait for guards arriving for work at 6.30am and then forced staff to reveal the security codes for the strongroom. Six Brinks Mat staff were handcuffed; one staff member was pistol-whipped over the head. Another was doused in petrol and threatened with being set alight. The security experts said that further robberies by high-technology criminals could be prevented with round-the-clock guards at bullion warehouses, remote surveillance and video screens to pick up movements around buildings, along with infrared spotlights and control over all people entering the trading estates where the warehouses were located. A special watch was immediately put on a handful of top crooks who were thought capable of pulling off the raid. The value of the haul, however, jumped by more than £1.1 million when the price of gold increased sharply in London, with some dealers claiming that the robbery had triggered the rise.

On 6ᵗʰ December 1983, a security guard was charged with taking part in the heist, while at least five other people were being questioned by police. A number of people were expected to be charged within the next two days. Anthony Black, a guard at the Brinks Mat warehouse, was remanded in custody for three days at Feltham Magistrates Court in Middlesex. The 31-year-old was arrested by Scotland Yard's Serious Crime Squad while the hunt for the haul continued, including gold bars, platinum, diamonds and travellers cheques. A number of items stolen in the heist were recovered in dawn raids on west London addresses prior to Black's arrest, but there was still no sign of the gold. Then, later in December, seven people in custody asked a high court judge to free them. The judge refused, but ordered the police to produce evidence to justify keeping the seven in custody. The application to release the prisoners was made by counsel Victor Durand, QC, after his clients were kept in custody for around 30 hours but refused a solicitor in all cases. Being detained at the time were 32-year-old John McAvoy and his wife Jacqueline, 29, Anthony White, 45, and his wife Margaret, 27, Patricia Dalligan, 43, and her sons, Mark, 17, and Stephen, 23.

In January 1984, 10 of the gold bars stolen in the robbery were believed to have turned up in Austria; they were seized by police in a raid on a hotel near Vienna Airport in which four Italians and an Austrian were arrested. The serial numbers were the same as those stolen in the robbery, but a police spokesman did state that the bars could be forged and used to dupe underworld buyers. In February that year, Anthony Black became a target for underworld criminals when it was discovered that he had "shopped" his accomplices. Police feared that there was a £1 million contract out on his life and he was advised by an Old Bailey judge that he would never again feel safe. Black confessed to his inside role in the robbery and was jailed for six years – a more lenient sentence due to the fact that he helped police. He was driven by armed police to a safe house, where he was to stay under 24-hour guard until he gave evidence against three other men, including McAvoy, White and 40-year-old Brian Robinson (at trials scheduled for three months later). After that, Black would be sent to jail.

In October 1984, a court heard how a security guard was so frightened by raiders that he forgot the combination to the safe. The man was doused in petrol and threatened with being set alight. In addition, he was threatened with being shot and having his penis cut off if he failed to remember the combination. However, the threats just made the man even more scared and he was eventually stabbed in the hand by the gang before he remembered the combination. Another man, Robin Riseley, was punched as the gang left after the raid – and told that "it was a good job it was Christmas".

McAvoy and Robinson were convicted of robbery by a jury sitting at the Old Bailey, but the police were still baffled about what had happened to the huge treasure trove of gold, jewels and cheques, and who the men's accomplices were. Detectives believed that the haul remained in Britain, and were hopeful that the raiders would break their silence to try to get off with lighter sentences. The four-week trial had been underpinned with a huge security operation, including police marksmen guarding the Old Bailey. When Black gave evidence, he was flanked by armed detectives, having turned "supergrass". Anthony White, however, was cleared of being involved. The two convicted men were each given 25 years.

By the end of January 1985, nearly 100lbs of gold worth £400,000 had been found by detectives hunting the stolen bullion. The gold and a diamond necklace were discovered in raids in London, Kent and the West Country, with the metal cast into rough bars to make it difficult to identify. Further swoops were then made on jewellers' shops and bullion offices, and a special helicopter joined the operation. The helicopter, fitted with heat-seeking equipment and powerful cameras, could spot areas where digging had taken place or where something might have been buried. It was brought in to cover the grounds of the luxury Hollywood Cottage in West Kingsdown, Kent, where undercover policeman John Fordham was stabbed to death. The country mansion was suspected of being the receiving base for the gold bullion; more than 22lbs of gold (worth £60,000) had already been found at the cottage and police believed that It came from the Brinks Mat robbery. Fordham was stabbed by builder Kenneth Noye, who told the police that Fordham should never have been on his property, although if he'd known he was a police officer he would not have stabbed him. Noye, 38, and Brian Reader, 45, were accused of murdering father-of-three, John Fordham.

At Lansdown, in Bath, police also dug up the grounds at the home of gold-dealer John Palmer. In addition, a corrugated iron and earthen smelter, along with small traces of gold, were also discovered. Palmer denied that he had any knowledge or involvement in the case and said that he had been holidaying with his family in Tenerife. He also accused the police of overreacting when they raided his home.

In March 1986, newspapers were full of runaway goldsmith John Palmer, who was accused of building a multi-pound fortune on his island refuge. He was wanted by Scotland Yard in connection with the robbery and Palmer knew that his days on the island were numbered. After the family holiday, a year earlier, his wife Marnie and their children had returned home, but Palmer stayed on in Tenerife in order to launch a timeshare project with London businessman Terry McKay. Palmer told reporters that he funded the project by selling his businesses in the UK.

Next in the dock was millionaire Noye, who was reported to have filed for legal aid stating that he: "Hasn't got a bean." The bullion smuggler was jailed for 14 years for his part in the Brinks Mat robbery, in which he made at least £3 million for fencing gold. The money had been frozen by the courts, although Noye had also got a fortune in foreign bank accounts. In August 1986, John "Goldfinger" Palmer was back behind bars following his return to the UK (after being refused entry to Brazil) and subsequently arrested and charged with conspiring along with Noye, Reader and seven others to dishonestly handle stolen gold bullion. He had melted down huge quantities of the gold and then sold it back to unsuspecting owners. Noye sent the gold from his home to Palmer's house – transported by Christopher Weyman who kept a secret record of every trip – where "Goldfinger" then melted it down to sell in Sheffield.

It then transpired in March 1987 that £13 million from the bullion robbery passed over the counter of a small country bank branch before police were alerted. Eventually, so many new notes were supplied in one month that the Bank of England had to tell the Treasury. Accountants, tax experts, solicitors and money managers also became involved to help launder and "invest" the proceeds. The money was invested in London and would have produced spectacular profits, but all this was successfully stopped when the money was secured in a holding account until all the court trials were finished, when it would then be claimed by insurers. Other avenues for laundering the money included allegedly passing £1 million in cash through the hands of John Fleming onto investment brokers. The 46-year-old south Londoner had emmigrated to Spain towards the end of 1983 but was on the run in South America by the beginning of 1987. After failing to find a safe haven, Fleming was deported by a US judge in Miami and returned to Britain in handcuffs.

At the beginning of April 1987 Palmer was sensationally cleared of being involved in the robbery. It was the first "not guilty" verdict given in the case and many of those in the public gallery screamed at the jury's decision. His acquittal meant that he could, once again, go back to a life of luxury. Fleming was also freed by the court two months later when a magistrate ruled that there wasn't enough evidence to send him for trial. A smiling Fleming stepped form London's Horseferry Road Court, having been in the dock accused of handling nearly £1 million in cash after the robbery. Disappointed Scotland Yard chiefs vowed to continue with their enquiries.

In October 1989 armed police arrested five people in their relentless search to solve the mystery surrounding the gold robbery. The dawn swoop was a major breakthrough in the six-year hunt for the Heathrow bullion robbers. Raids on nine homes in London, Kent and Surrey were made by 60 officers from Scotland Yard's Special Task Force. Later, they froze a sophisticated international network of bank accounts holding £16.2 million. The money was said to be proceeds from the gold bars taken during the robbery, interest on accounts and "dirty" money from other crimes. Until the raids, only £10.5 million had been recovered from the robbery.

Knightsbridge Security Deposit Robbery

(1987)

The headlines in the press on 14th July 1987 read: "Ice cool thieves robbed Britain's wealthiest people of more than £20 million in just one hour after bluffing their way into a top security bank vault". The men, wearing dark business suits, posed as potential customers after making an appointment and asking to see the security arrangements. Once inside, they pulled out a sawn-off shotgun and a hand gun, handcuffed two guards and a manager, and cleared out 113 safe-deposit boxes. They held a gun to the head of the manager while they jemmied open the biggest of the 4,000 boxes in the vault and stuffed the contents into sacks.

Carried out on 12th July 1987, in Knightsbridge, London, the robbery is said to be one of the biggest in the world. The raid was organized and implemented by Italian Valerio Viccei, a lawyer's son who was already wanted for at least 50 armed robberies in his native country. He had fled from Italy to London in order to avoid arrest and, once in the capital, resumed a life of crime in order to pay for his playboy lifestyle.

At the time of the robbery, it was feared that the true scale of the crime would never be realized as owners of the safe-deposit boxes were not required to reveal what they had lost. However, one victim, Rosemary Robertson, was happy to reveal her losses. The robbery took place at the Knightsbridge Safe Deposit Centre opposite Harrods, where the raid on the vault went without the slightest hitch. Many of the country's richest people used the top-security centre, which was described as the most secure in the world. As many of the safe-deposit boxes contained sensitive documents, it was feared that some victims could be open to blackmail from the robbers. A police spokesman said at the time: "The staff did not consider it unusual when the men asked to see the vault. It was normal. And, the men certainly looked the part of wealthy businessmen in their dark suits and suntans."

The deposit centre was opened four years before the robbery in a blaze of publicity. Its owners were sure it was the "best in the world", designed to deter even the most hardened criminals. But this was not enough to stop Viccei and his gang, who found that the strongroom had 2ft thick steel walls and an entrance protected by armed security guards, surrounded by bulletproof glass. Infrared heat and sound detectors were also installed, designed to pick up the smallest movement. Each customer was issued with personalized coded cards to gain entry to the vaults but, despite the high security, the simplicity of the raid left the owners of the centre extremely embarrassed.

Rosemary Robertson, 45, the daughter of jewellery tycoon Algernon Asprey, lost family heritage worth "hundreds of thousands of pounds", and said: "I'm devastated. We've lost a lot. I just never thought it could happen here. It seemed so safe. I've had my jewellery and silver in there since it opened because I don't feel safe with it at home. I was

Louvre – Mona Lisa (1911) Leonardo Da Vinci's Mona Lisa was stolen from the Louvre in Paris in 1911 as part of an audacious plan by con man Eduardo de Valfierno.

The scene in the Louvre shows the vacant space where the bewitching smile of the Mona Lisa had previously hung, and the four hooks that were the sole means of securing the priceless 16th-century painting.

Page 8   THE DAILY MIRROR

VACANT SPACE IN THE LOUVRE WHERE THE LOST 'MONA LISA' HUNG.

Houndsditch Murders (1910) An attempted robbery at HS Harris Jewellers in December 1910 led to unbelievable events over the next few weeks, culminating in 200 police officers cordoning off an area of Stepney after a tip-off that members of the gang were hiding out in one of the houses in Sidney Street.

Croydon Aerodrome (1935) First opened in March 1920, Croydon Aerodrome provided the backdrop for a successful heist that resulted in a haul of more than £20,000 (worth £12 million today) that was never recovered.

Eastcastle Street (1952) Billy Hill was the leader of the gang suspected to be behind the robbery of a GPO van in Eastcastle Street in May 1952. The crooks stole registered mail believed to be valued at more than £40,000.

Derek Bentley and Christopher Craig (1952) Exhibits to be used in the trial of Derek Bentley and Christopher Craig are brought into court, December 1952.

Christopher Craig (aged 16) is brought into court on an ambulance stretcher. Craig was found guilty of shooting and killing policeman Sidney Miles during a robbery in November 1952. On account of his youth, Craig was remanded to prison while his accomplice, 19-year-old Derek Bentley, was hanged for his involvement.

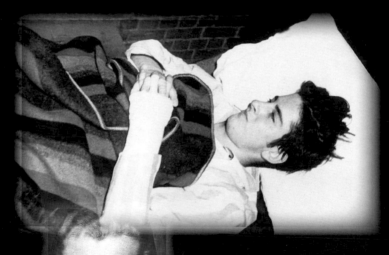

Derek Bentley was hanged on 28th January 1953 for his involvement in the death of policeman Sidney Miles. The case quickly became a rallying cry for the abolition of corporal punishment.

Great Train Robbery (1963) An aerial shot of Sears Crossing where the Great Train Robbers took charge of the train in August 1963.

Leatherslade Farm at Oakley in Buckinghamshire was the gang's hideout in the immediate aftermath of the Great Train Robbery.

Ronnie Biggs is escorted into court in September 1963. He was found guilty of conspiracy to rob and armed robbery and was sentenced to 30 years, but served just 19 months before escaping.

The route taken by Great Train Robber Ronnie Biggs on his escape from Wandsworth Prison in July 1965.

UP ESCAPE LADDERS

THROUGH TRAPDOOR IN ROOF

ON TO VAN FLOOR

INTO GETAWAY CARS

Lloyds, Baker Street, London (1971) Police inspect the burglar alarm at Lloyds Bank in Baker Street, the scene of the Walkie-Talkie Bank Raid in September 1971.

Security Express (1983) Ronnie Knight, pictured with his then wife, actress Barbara Windsor, spent many years in exile in Spain before returning to Britain to face justice for the raid on Security Express in April 1983.

Brinks Mat Bullion Raid (1983) The Brinks Mat Security Depot at Heathrow from which three tons of gold bars were stolen in November 1983.

Security guard Anthony Black was the inside man on the Brinks Mat gold bullion robbery at Heathrow.

John Palmer may have been cleared of any alleged involvement in the Brinks Mat heist but in May 2001 was found guilty of a £30 million timeshare fraud.

ARE YOUR VALUABLES SAFE
AT HOME OR IN THE OFFICE!

There are 500 recorded break-ins
every day in London.

SECURITY DEPOSITS PLC
OFFERS YOU:

• Your own private Safe Deposit
  Box from £99 per annum inc. VAT

• Open 7 days a week
  8am to 8pm Mon to Sat
  10am to 5pm Sun & Bank Holiday

• No Waiting

• No extra charges for visits

• Insurance Cover of £25,000 on
  an "All Risks" Basis (excluding
  cash or currency) at no extra cost

SECURITY DEPOSITS

1-6 Brompton Road   16/18 Circus Road
Knightsbridge   St. Johns Wood
London SW3 1HX   London NW8 6PG
01-581 1212   01-586 9431

Knightsbridge Security Deposit Robbery (1987) This advertising campaign aimed to persuade the public that their valuables would be safer if they were entrusted to a Safe Deposit Box. Ironically, the Knightsbridge Safe Deposit Centre was the victim of a daring armed robbery in July 1987.

A crowd of concerned people assembles outside the Safe Deposit Centre after news of the robbery is released.

Italian Valerio Viccei (left) led the armed robbery at the Knightsbridge Safe Deposit Centre when his gang broke into 126 boxes and got away with an estimated £40 million.

The damage inside the Safe Deposit Centre reveals numerous boxes broken and scattered during the robbery.

Exhibits Officer DC Steve Ashcroft with the £4.5 million Flick diamond and other goods recovered from the robbery.

Millennium Dome (2000) Such was the accuracy of the police intelligence that the would-be robbers were caught on camera in their JCB and van en route to the Millennium Dome in November 2000.

William Cockram and Ray Betson are photographed testing the getaway speedboat weeks before the robbery.

Robert Alvin Adams (left) is captured on film attacking the cabinet that housed the Millennium Star diamond with a sledgehammer.

The scene inside the Millennium Dome showing the JCB used in the attempted robbery raid of the Millennium jewels.

The gang's intended target was the Millennium jewels, 11 rare blue diamonds.

Graff Jewellery Heist, Mayfair (2004 and 2009) The prestigious Graff jewellery store in Mayfair has been the target of more than one robbery. In 2004 Pedja Vujosevic and his fellow criminals got away with an estimated £23 million haul during a three-minute raid.

Victor Lustig (Eiffel Tower Scam, 1925) Completed in 1889, the Eiffel Tower has been a Parisian icon ever since. But it has also been "sold" twice for scrap metal by con artist Victor Lustig on two separate, but related occasions.

John Haigh (1944–49) John George Haigh was a self-confessed serial killer who murdered nine victims in the 1940s for financial gain.

A large crowd gathers outside 79 Gloucester Road, where detectives are investigating the disappearance of Mrs Durand Deacon in March 1949.

Dr Archibald Henderson, his wife Rosalie Henderson (below left) and Mrs Durand-Deacon (below right): three people who fell victim to John Haigh, aka the Acid Bath Murderer.

Detectives search for remains in the grounds of a factory in Crawley as they hunt for clues relating to murderer John Haigh.

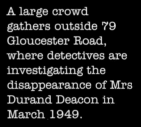

3 deaths

VE P
AS
-Q.C.
GES

Dr. JOHN BODKIN ADAMS—Sitting by the desk in his surgery at Trinity Trees, Eastbourne, Sussex.

Dr. Adams poisoned widow with drugs, says Crown

'In a Coma'

Mind Clear

'Pretended'

WHAT IT'S ABOUT

DR. JOHN BODKIN ADAMS, 57, of Eastbourne, is accused of murdering a widow, Mrs. Edith Alice Morrell, 81, by poisoning her with drugs.

THE CASE OF ALFRED HULLETT

'Expected More'

THE CASE OF GERTRUDE HULLETT

'Dark Corner'

'Rich Patient'

'Not Yet Dead'

Dr John Bodkin Adams (1956) Dr John Bodkin Adams, pictured sitting at the desk in his surgery at Trinity Trees, Eastbourne, Sussex.

The funeral of Edith Alice Morrell takes place in November 1950. The wealthy widow was a victim of suspected serial killer Dr John Bodkin Adams, who benefited from her will.

Guinness Share-trading Fraud (1986) Sir Jack Lyons (left) and Ernest Saunders (below), two of the men convicted after their involvement in the Guinness takeover battle.

Robert Maxwell and the Missing Millions (1991) Robert
Maxwell with Prime Minister Margaret Thatcher during
her visit to the *Daily Mirror* offices in March 1985, just
six years before his death prompted an investigation into
missing millions.

One year's Nick

I've done the best deal of my life grins guilty trader Leeson

ROGUE trader Nick Leeson faced a likely maximum year in jail last night – and reckoned he'd pulled off the best deal in his life.

Grinning Leeson admitted two charges of fraud when he appeared in court in Singapore yesterday for his part in the £860million collapse of Barings Bank earlier this year.

By MARK DOWDNEY Foreign Editor

Nine other charges were dropped after he agreed to co-operate with investigators and pay 70,000 prosecution costs.

It is now believed the trader will receive only a two or three-year jail term. Instead of a maximum eight years, when he is sentenced today.

With time off for good behaviour, and the nine months he has already been held, he could be free in months.

Leeson, 28, smiled and joked through yesterday's brief hearing.

He was relaxed enough to send out for a lunch of two burgers, a cola and chips.

And he laughed when he learned that his cheque for costs had fallen short by £740 because of an overnight fluctuation in currencies.

Disastrous

Prosecutors do not believe he acted alone in breaking 233-year-old Barings – Britain's oldest merchant bank – by disastrous trading.

Yesterday they claimed in court that the bank's two most senior executives in Singapore –

James Bax and Simon Jones – knew of cash discrepancies but did nothing to raise the alarm.

Both men and Peter Norris, chief of Barings' investment arm in Britain, have already been singled out in a report by investigators.

Leeson's lawyer, John Koh, also claimed that executives in London knew what was going on.

He told the court: "At one point, my client was encouraged to mislead auditors."

Mr Koh stressed that Leeson did not profit from his activities.

He said there would be NO Hollywood movie and revealed proceeds from a £450,000 book deal would go to agents and lawyers. He said: "My client is not

a crook. He is extremely remorseful. There are no secret profits and he has no assets."

Leeson's wife Lisa, 27, suffered a miscarriage about a month before the trader fled Singapore, it was revealed yesterday.

She will not see her husband sentenced.

After flying back to Britain, she is staying with friends at an unknown address. Her father Alec Sims, of West Kingsdown, Kent, said: "She is under stress."

CONVICTED: Leeson admitted two counts of fraud

Nick Leeson (1995) Rogue trader Nick Leeson admitted two charges of fraud when he appeared in court in Singapore for his part in the £860 million collapse of Barings Bank in 1995.

afraid of raiders." None of the Asprey jewellery was insured.

Following the raid, police were desperately trying to find the owners of the raided safe-deposit boxes while they also wanted to interview anyone who was near the centre at the time of the robbery. The alarm was raised an hour after the incident at 6.45pm – after the raiders had got away – when the staff managed to pick their handcuffs free with paper clips. However, this wasn't the end of the gripping scenes at the centre.

The same day as the newspaper reports, angry customers descended on the centre on Tuesday 14th July 1987 and demanded to know if they had been robbed. There were chaotic scenes as customers tried to battle their way into the centre. Most were furious that security at the centre had been breached and one said: "How could it happen? We were told it was the most secure strongroom in the world." The customer went on: "But when I walked in off the street to ask about their services I was not searched or asked for any identification. Within minutes I was being shown around the vaults and how their security system worked." By this time, it was known that at least one person had lost £5 million. Another victim was a member of the fabulously wealthy Saudi royal family, who was stunned by the loss. The royal had lost art treasure and irreplaceable Cartier jewels, while an American businessman who found his box intact put things into perspective by saying: "Although the place is dynamite proof and H-bomb proof it does not matter at all. If someone comes up and puts a shotgun in your face you are not going to die for someone else's deposit box." One Kensington housewife lost her entire life savings.

Basically, the vault had been a "sitting duck".

An undercover journalist found the centre easy to access even following the robbery. "Inside information" that could have contributed to the robbers getting away with their easy pickings was still freely available in the days after the raid. The detailed layout of the Knightsbridge strongroom was actually on public show at Kensington Town Hall – just a mile away – it was discovered. The journalist visited the Town Hall in the aftermath and talked to a helpful woman official in the planning department, who told him all he wanted to know without even asking his name. At first the woman had appeared nervy, but when the man confirmed he was a member of the public, she brightened and agreed to show him the plans of the centre, which were kept on microfilm on the third floor of the Town Hall. The woman readily set up the microfilm on a screen and, to the journalist's amazement, a wealth of sensitive information flashed before his eyes.

The intricate plan – one hundredth of the real thing – showed two security offices, exit routes (including fire escapes and stairs), details of smoke vents and ramps and the strength of the strongroom door, which was 600mm thick. The journalist wasn't allowed to obtain a copy of the plan. However, he was left alone in the room with the microfilm for a full 15 minutes, when he could easily have taken a photograph. He browsed over the plan and took notes – which were permitted – before he left unnoticed without even having to sign out.

It had taken two heavily suntanned men in business suits (and their accomplices) just one hour to ransack the security vaults after bluffing their way in. Business at the centre continued to be brisk, and plans of the layout of the vault were still available to members of the public, despite the massive raid. Security plans were to be stepped up, yet if anyone wanted to inspect the strongroom that was still possible. Plans of Buckingham Palace and the Bank of England are classified, so why weren't the plans of the security vaults?

The robbers might have been brazen, and they might have been lucky when their simple plan worked, but it seemed that they weren't as clever as they thought when a fortune in jewels stolen in the £20 million raid were found stored in safe-deposit boxes. The thieves – who were suspected of having Mafia connections – took their loot to another London vault to try to keep it safe. Three pieces of the recovered jewellery, found in early August 1987 (less than a month after the robbery), were said to be worth £3 million. Police believed that the rest – including silver and cash – was worth a further £4 million, and the hunt continued for the remainder of the stolen property. Some had been found in cars, hotel rooms and houses in London. Nine suspects, including four Italians, were held and questioned by police.

Senior officers were convinced that the raid had been planned in Italy after an underworld tip-off gave them their first major clue. The tip-off was possibly prompted by anger that "outsiders" had pulled off the robbery, as it was believed that some of the stolen loot had been placed in the safe-deposit boxes by British thieves. The big breakthrough came as police were keeping watch on an Italian suspect at White's Hotel in London's Bayswater Road. When an officer tried to arrest him, the suspect attempted to flee at high-speed in a Ferrari, but the car was rammed by police and the Italian was eventually arrested after a violent struggle. Meanwhile, two other Italians were arrested following a car chase in Mayfair. After the three were questioned, six other people – including a woman – were arrested in late-night raids. All nine were held separately in police stations across London. Commander Jerry Plowman, who led the month-long hunt by 60 officers from the Flying Squad and the Intelligence Branch, said: "Ironically, we are recovering property from other safety boxes and extensive inquiries are going to try and find more."

Owners who lost valuables were being asked to come forward to identify their property but, in August 1987, only 80 had responded to the police appeal. By then, it appeared that police were dealing with a raid that amounted to more than £30 million in stolen property and cash. The value of the loot recovered had reached "silly money" according to a Flying Squad boss. In the next swoop at a north London house, silver and gems worth several million pounds were recovered and two people appeared in court on 14th August 1987 in connection with the raid. Stephen Mann, aged 38, an Abbey Life insurance associate, was charged with robbery and remanded in custody while Helle Skoubon, 29, an assistant manager of a fashion shop, was accused of dishonestly handling cash and jewellery worth £10,000.

In November 1988, the gunman who masterminded the raid (eventually totalled at £40 million), Valerio Viccei, faced a packed courtroom at the Old Bailey, who were told how he had so much of the loot from the robbery that he had filled his bath with money. Viccei had allegedly been so excited by the raid that he boasted it was: "the most fantastic robbery of all time!" The gang had used sledgehammers to smash open 120 boxes at the deposit centre, where they hung a notice on the front door claiming the centre was shut for a short time – so that they wouldn't be disturbed. The note apologized to customers for any "inconvenience caused during improvements to our security system", and ended with the words, "Business as usual tomorrow". However, the jury were told that Viccei left vital clues in the vault, which was strewn with leftover gold and jewels, including a bloody fingerprint and prints on two newspapers. The Italian had been arrested along with four other men within a month of the raid. Detectives found a pistol and bullets in a safe-deposit box rented by Viccei along with £52,000 in cash and 500,000 Swiss francs. During investigations it had become clear that the centre's owner, Pakistani businessman Parves Latif, had allegedly helped set up the robbery as an inside job. He owed his bank £50,000 and the business was £470,000 in the red. Shortly before the raid, Latif doubled his robbery insurance. Viccei, 33, and Latif, 31, both denied the robbery as did three others from the gang. Four of the accused also denied firearms charges. However, one man, antiques dealer Israel Pinkas, admitted handling some of the stolen property.

After two months of trial, Viccei – the swaggering gunman who wore dark sunglasses and cracked jokes throughout the proceedings – was found guilty of the robbery and sentenced to 22 years behind bars. However, it was believed that the Italian had £30 million stashed away; he afforded the judge a sly smile as he was sentenced. Viccei had been caught after flashing his money around and a string of blunders. He had been planning on moving to Columbia if he hadn't been snared by police at a location where he was planning to open a safety deposit centre and then rob it. The jury had taken 26 hours in their deliberations over Viccei and three other gang members, who were also convicted. Latif was jailed for 18 years while 48-year-old David Poole got 16 years. Pamela Seamarks, the former lover of both the womanizing Viccei and Latif, was given an 18-month suspended sentence for handling £50,000 from the robbery and for stealing £15,000. Supergrass Stephen Mann, who gave evidence against the gang, was jailed for five years after appearing in court with a broken nose and smashed teeth following a beating by inmates at Wandsworth Prison. His counsel told the court that Mann was a "marked man". The blunders by the gang – which led to their eventual downfall – included Viccei cutting himself and leaving a bloody fingerprint while smashing up boxes, using flimsy handcuffs that were easily picked with a paper clip and cheap walkie-talkies that broke down. As £30 million of the raid was never recovered and the owners of the boxes didn't come forward, police believed that the loot was the proceeds of drug smuggling and robberies.

The single most valuable item in the haul was the Flick diamond – as big as the palm of a hand – worth £4.5 million at the time of the robbery. It was sold by Viccei "under the counter" in Antwerp for almost £1 million, but a Flying Squad officer got it back for just £300,000 using the thief's own money. The Italian had told a dealer in Belgium that he had inherited the gem and wanted to avoid Italian taxes. He accepted a low price when it was offered in US dollars via a bank in Luxembourg. Later, Detective Inspector Dick Leach flew to the Continent with a suitcase full of Viccei's cash and pulled off a coup that won the admiration of his London bosses. He persuaded the dealer to part with the Flick diamond – and four smaller stones – in return for his legal commission alone. Parts of the haul that remained unclaimed were put on display at Scotland Yard and, after a year, were auctioned with the proceeds going to the Police Property Fund, Boys' Clubs and welfare organizations in deprived inner-London areas.

In April 2000, playboy mobster Viccei died in a shoot-out with police. He was killed on an isolated dirt track in Italy as he plotted his next criminal exploit with a well-known Mafia figure. He was on day-release from jail, following extradition from Britain after serving five years of his 22-year sentence. It was believed that Viccei and Antonio Maletesta were planning a serious crime at the time they were stopped in a stolen Lancia Thema by police.

City Bond Theft, London

(1990)

A mugger fled with £300 million on 2nd May 1990, but police claimed he'd never be able to spend a single penny of it. The knife-wielding bandit pulled off the world's biggest mugging when he grabbed a briefcase from a terrified money-firm messenger. Inside the case were certificates of deposit with a face value of £121,900,000 and Treasury bills worth £170 million. But, the Bank of England said it would be extraordinarily difficult to cash the bonds. The thief could have tried to present them when they expired, sell them on the market, or use them as security to raise a loan, but in each case it seemed he would be doomed to failure as he would have had to prove that he was entitled to them. Banks around the world were already on the lookout for the "hot" certificates.

The certificates of deposit were issued to companies in exchange for depositing money with a finance house, while Treasury bills are a form of IOU issued by the government to raise short-term money. At the time of the robbery, a City expert said: "It wouldn't be easy for anyone to walk in off the street and leave with a sack full of cash." The raider had struck in broad daylight as 58-year-old messenger John Goddard was walking from one money house to another in the City of London. Police issued a photofit of the wanted man – described as in his 20s – as the mugging meant that a fortune was missing from the

City's money stock, forcing the Bank of England to step in with £300 million worth of aid. It was reported in the press how billions of pounds are "walked" around the City each day, and there were plans to tighten security and transfer documents by computer instead.

On 16th May 1990, a crook tried to cash a money bond stolen during the mugging, and financial houses were warned that further attempts would probably be made. By the end of the month, three men had been arrested in connection with the robbery after customs officers stumbled on £77 million worth of stolen securities during a routine baggage search. The documents were unearthed at Heathrow Airport, where they had been transferred from Dublin to London aboard a British Airways flight. The 80 certificates of deposit were undoubtedly part of the haul. In September 1990, more customs officials probing international money laundering grabbed £71 million worth of bank bonds in Miami, which meant that nearly all the bonds stolen had been recovered. In fact, all but two of the bonds were found, thanks to an informant and the infiltration of City of London police and the FBI into the gang involved in laundering the bonds.

John Goddard, a messenger with money broker Sheppards, had been mugged at knifepoint in a quiet side street at 9.30am. He had been subjected to a brutal and terrifying mugging for £300 million that was worthless on the street. Police strongly believed that Patrick Thomas, a petty thief, was responsible for the actual mugging but he was never charged. He was found dead with a gunshot wound to his head in December 1991. Keith Cheeseman was sentenced to six and a half years for his part in the robbery, while four others were also charged. No evidence was brought against Cheeseman's accomplices and they walked free from court following their trials in 1991.

Bank of France Robbery

(1992)

In a "human bomb" raid, robbers strapped sticks of dynamite between a security guard's legs and held him hostage in France's biggest-ever bank raid on 17th December 1992. Ten hooded raiders descended on the Toulon branch of the Bank of France and cleaned out safes for two hours – netting £37 million – before they ran out of sacks.

The gang, using inside information from an employee of the bank, had also kidnapped the guard's family before using him as a booby trap to carry out the raid. Once inside the bank, they removed film from the surveillance cameras. However, within two months of the raid, most of the gang were caught. A number of the gang escaped with most of the loot when the "inside" employee gave himself up to police along with the names of other gang members. All members of the gang who fled the authorities were convicted and sentenced, in absentia, to life imprisonment. Then, after 20 years on the run, Algerian Miloud Hai, aged 48, was caught.

Carlton Hotel, Cannes

(1994)

The InterContinental Carlton Hotel in Cannes, situated on the French Riviera, is listed as a National Historic Building. Built in 1911, the hotel is the most prestigious venue for those attending the annual Cannes Film Festival and is often the backdrop for deal-making in the motion picture industry. Its 343 luxury rooms provide the ideal setting for A-listers promoting their films during the world-renowned festival. However, in 1994, the Carlton became famous for a little more than its upmarket clientele and the film industry when it found itself at the centre of a jewellery robbery.

The scene of Grace Kelly's first meeting with Prince Rainier III of Monaco and the film setting for Hitchcock's *To Catch A Thief* was spiralled into a world of violence and robbery when three thieves burst into the hotel. Their intention was to rob the hotel's jewellery store just as it was closing. Firing machine guns, the robbers intimidated staff and made off with around £30 million worth of jewels. While it transpired that they had been firing blanks, they left no clues behind as to their identities and neither the jewels nor the gang were ever traced.

Midland Bank Clearing Centre in Salford, Greater Manchester

(1995)

Masked gunmen left behind £4 million on 3rd July 1995 after snatching £6 million in a daring 10-minute raid. The loot was left behind because it was likely too heavy for the four raiders who could not carry all the cash. They decided to cut their losses at the Midland Bank Clearing Centre in Salford, Greater Manchester, after holding a gun to the head of the driver of a Securicor van at the service centre. The gang forced him to drive the vehicle, which was loaded with money for hundreds of cash machines, to a quiet back street just two minutes from a police station. The driver was then handcuffed to railings while the gang stuffed 29 bags of cash into the back of a stolen white van. But, with their van nearly full and the alarm about to be raised, they decided to flee leaving a substantial amount behind. The Securicor vehicle was hijacked as it approached the service centre in Regent Place, Salford, during the morning rush hour, and was later found abandoned in Hope Street. The alarm was raised by a workman who saw the guard being handcuffed. Police chiefs agreed that the raid in broad daylight during a busy period was daring; a police spokesman confirmed that the raid was probably the biggest ever in Greater Manchester at the time.

The Securicor driver and ex-policeman, Graham Huckerby, went on to enjoy a jet-set lifestyle after his security van was robbed – and found himself in court in May 2001 accused of being the "inside" man in the heist. The jury heard how the then 41-year-old took a bribe to allow the masked gunmen to hijack his bulletproof, bomb-proof vehicle, and how after the incident he managed to pay off debts and take holidays. The gang had snatched £4 million in cash and more than £2 million in cheques. The cash was still missing at the time of the court case and the robbers were yet to be traced. Huckerby, however, denied the charges and was adamant that he had been kidnapped. But on 14th March 2002 he was found guilty and convicted of being involved in the robbery. He was jailed for 14 years in April that same year. He had taken a bribe to let the gunmen hijack his armoured van and stage a fake kidnapping. The gang tied up Huckerby and gagged him before making off with the loot. It later transpired that the ex-policeman had been paid £2,500 for his part in the heist and had not been "terrified" when his vehicle was hijacked. Huckerby, of Prestwich, Greater Manchester, came under suspicion when undercover officer "Barry" joined Securicor and found that the suspect had paid off maintenance arrears, taken a holiday in California, made £500 bank deposits and given his then 12-year-old daughter a number of gifts. Huckerby's "handler", 60-year-old James Power, was also jailed for 14 years by Minshull Street Crown Court. Both men were convicted of conspiracy to rob.

Millennium Dome

(2000)

Three weeks before the foiled robbery at the Millennium Dome in London in 2000, the same gang – dubbed the "River Rats" due to their choice of getaway on the river – gave up on an attempt to raid the Dome. The robbery was abandoned because they could not get their getaway boat to start. However, on 7th November 2000, they tried again and used a JCB digger to ram their way into the Dome's Money Zone, aiming to steal the gems on display.

But the gang were arrested before they could snatch a world-record £350 million worth of gems, including the 203-carat Millennium Star diamond. Detective Superintendent Jon Shatford said: "It was an audacious attempt but was met by an even more audacious response." The raiders brandished sledgehammers and powerful nail guns and, while wearing protective gas masks, set off smoke grenades. But Scotland Yard detectives, who had been watching them for months, swooped on the four startled intruders and captured the speedboat they planned to escape in. Others were arrested nearby and, on the day of the raid, 12 people were held. All were questioned about two other crimes in which blundering crooks tried to net nearly £20 million. They fled empty handed.

The gang's final preparations for the planned raid three weeks earlier were closely monitored by specialist police officers. But, when the robbers tried to move their speedboat to a pier alongside the

Dome, the engine refused to fire. They tinkered with it for half an hour then gave up and went home. The other botched raids about which the suspects were quizzed took place at Nine Elms in south London and Aylesford in Kent. At Nine Elms, the raiders were foiled by a local resident who took the ignition keys from their ram truck because he objected to it being parked outside his home. In Aylesford, they failed to get into an armoured truck carrying £10 million because they knocked out its hydraulic systems. As a result, the tail-lift couldn't be lowered.

At 9.40am on the morning of 7th November 2000, the 10-ton JCB digger hurtled through the wall of the Millennium Dome carrying the raiders. It was the start of what was planned as the world's biggest robbery. As astonished visitors looked on, the armed raiders – wearing gas masks and bulletproof vests – hurled five smoke grenades as they raced for their fabulous prize in the vaults of the Money Zone. Once at the target, they feverishly attacked the 2in armoured glass protecting the priceless Millennium Star and 11 other diamonds with sledgehammers and industrial nail guns, but what they didn't know was that the daring mission had been betrayed weeks earlier and the gems switched for crystal imitations. And, as the men pounded at the glass, they were surrounded by 100 Flying Squad sharpshooters who had been lying in wait; many were disguised as Dome cleaners. Reeling in disbelief, the bungling raiders had no choice but to surrender without a shot being fired.

Delighted at the outcome, Shatford said: "They [the raiders] were overwhelmed by numbers." There was nothing they could do, he added. In a Bond-like scene, one raider was arrested as he tried to flee down the Thames in a high-powered getaway speedboat, while another man was held on the opposite bank of the Thames, where he was waiting in a getaway van. Six others were seized after two swoops on properties in Kent owned by a family of scrap metal dealers.

The raid had been planned since the summer of 2000. The flawless Millennium Star, owned by De Beers, was obviously the target and it was believed that the "River Rats" had already arranged a buyer for the jewels in the diamond markets of New York and Hong Kong. The Millennium Star had been mined in the Congo in the early 1990s; it is 2in long and had taken three years to cut and polish. It went on display at the Dome along with other blue diamonds in September 1999. The value of the diamond was listed to be priceless, although it was insured for £350 million.

A senior Scotland Yard source confirmed that the jewels would have been hidden in Britain for a few months before being smuggled out of the country one by one. Detectives were first tipped off about the raid nearly two months previously and had been following the gang ever since. They had no idea about which day the gang planned to strike, but had earmarked 25 possible days. On the eve of each "danger" day, the gems were replaced by "dummies".

Wearing workmen's jackets, the robbers waved their way past security guards before crashing through the Dome's blue perimeter fence. Crushing a bollard, the digger powered across Millennium Way, up a ramp and through a double set of steel gates towards the left-hand side of the building. A sharp right turn then sent the raiders towards the panel wall of the main exhibition area. Only 64 visitors, including children from three schools, were inside the Dome at the time. Outside the Dome, following the foiled raid, police cars and vans screeched to a halt with sirens blazing while a helicopter hovered overhead.

The gang's dreams of wealth had disappeared as they were led out of the Dome one by one with their hands on their heads. They were then ordered to lie on the ground with police rifles trained on them before being handcuffed and taken away to police stations in south London.

Despite the success of police to foil the robbers, there was talk about whether or not the Dome staff and schoolchildren visiting the site were in danger while the raid and subsequent arrests were carried out. One head teacher, Elizabeth Lutzeier, was particularly angered that 29 children from her school were allowed into the Dome as armed police lay in wait. However, Shatford was firm in his response, saying that because the police waited until the raiders had entered the vault and, in so doing, trapped themselves, the officers had done the right thing – and no members of the public were at risk at any time.

On 8th November 2001, a packed court at the Old Bailey was told how the operation was planned professionally, carefully and down to the last detail. It was so well organized that the gang would probably have got away with it if it hadn't been for an equally professional police operation. The accused included charter skipper Kevin Meredith, aged 34, Wayne Taylor, 35, Aldo Ciarrochi, 31, William Cockram, 48, Robert Adams, 57, and Ray Betson, 39. Four of the men were caught red-handed with the JCB in the Dome. Meredith was the speedboat driver, while Taylor played his part in planning what was going to happen. All six denied conspiracy to rob. The court also heard how 56-year-old Terence Millman was in a van on the other side of the Thames. He never made it to trial as he died before being brought before the court. On 4th December 2001, one of the accused, Kevin Meredith, joined Old Bailey judge Michael Coombe and the 12 jurors who were to decide his fate in a two-hour tour of the Dome to establish the details of the robbery: they were shown where the JCB had crashed into the building, and the jetty where the getaway boat was waiting.

On 18th February 2002, five men were jailed for their part in the raid. Gang leaders William Cockram and Ray Betson were given 18 years. Aldo Ciarrocchi and Robert Adams were both given 15 years. All admitted conspiracy to steal, but denied more serious charges of conspiracy to rob. But they were convicted by 10-2 verdicts after the jury deliberated for 35 hours at the end of the three-month trial. Meredith received five years. The judge told the five: "This was a very well-planned and premeditated attempt to rob De Beers of what would have been the most gigantic sum in English legal history – or any other, for that matter." He concluded: "This was a wicked plan, a professional plan and one which was carried out with the minutest attention to detail. Mercifully the police were on to it and the observations took place." In the words of the prosecutor, Martin Heslop, QC: "It could properly be described as the Robbery of the Millennium."

It was also suspected that the gang's two leaders had netted £20 million from four raids carried out before the Dome plot, but police had so far failed to nail Betson and Cockram over the daring robberies. Before their diamond dream, the two men had lived charmed lives, serving just short jail terms for minor offences. Betson owned a £500,000 home in Loos, Kent, and a £200,000 townhouse, plus top-of-the-range cars and he had spent a Christmas in New York, flying business class and staying in £500-a-night hotels along with Cockram and their respective partners. But, according to records, he had never done a day's work in his life. The previous heists committed by the two men were believed to have included grabbing cash from armoured trucks and cash depots in 1996 and 1997. Detectives thought that the money was shipped abroad, "laundered" through property deals and "invested" in bulk drug shipments to Britain.

Lee Wenham, a gofer for the gang, thought the Dome heist would be like the one in *The Italian Job*, starring Michael Caine, or something out of a James Bond film. The 33-year-old mechanic, who had a low IQ and a reading age of seven, gave a double thumbs-up to the judge as he was jailed for nine years in February 2002 after his part in the gang's exploits. According to his barrister, Wenham "was exploited by some very serious and sophisticated criminals and didn't have the intelligence or the experience to combat that". Wenham had allowed the Dome raiders to use family farms as hideouts, carried out reconnaissance and helped modify the JCB digger. Four months earlier, he had helped a gang led by Millman in a failed attempt to steal £9 million from a Securicor van in Aylesford, Kent. He was jailed for conspiracy to rob the Securicor van and was also given a concurrent sentence of four years for conspiracy to steal from the

Dome. Wenham admitted both charges.

Two years later, Betson was back in the press when it was announced in November 2004 that he was suing the prison where he was serving his time for limiting the number of phone calls he was allowed to make. Betson claimed that the limited phone calls were a breach of his human rights; he was only allowed to spend £11 a week on the phone. All his calls from Whitemoor Prison in Cambridgeshire were monitored, but it was thought that he had come up with a code to stop prison staff finding out what he was really talking about. Betson petitioned the high court, arguing that Governor Martin Lomas and Prison Service Chief Phil Wheatley cannot stop his calls; the mastermind behind the failed Dome heist wanted to be able to spend as much money as he liked calling people. He also wanted the court to downgrade him from a Category A prisoner – the most dangerous – so that he could have an easier time in prison. He had already appealed and managed to get his 18-year sentence reduced to 15 years.

Antwerp Diamond Heist

(2003)

More than £65 million worth of diamonds were stolen in the biggest heist to hit the diamond-cutting capital of the world on the 15th and 16th February 2003. Thieves made off with the massive haul of gems from Antwerp's diamond centre in Belgium, clearing out 123 of the 160 vaults in the maximum-security cellars over one weekend. Police believed that a gang operating with inside information pulled off the daring raid. The authorities arrived on the scene to find jewels scattered along the floor of the cellar as the gang had obviously dropped gems in their rush to get away with the multi-million-pound sting.

Two days after the heist, officers and traders were still baffled by how it could have happened, as there was no sign of a break-in and the centre was surrounded by security cameras. Detectives did, however, suspect it was an inside job because it would have taken hours to empty the 123 vaults. Officers struggled to put a price on the losses, but almost £3 million of diamonds were stolen when just five vaults were cleared in 1993. Youri Steverlynck of the diamond council said at the time: "We are certainly talking about many millions. We will have to see to what extent the security system failed." Meanwhile, city prosecutor, Leen Nuyts said: "Staff are being questioned."

What the authorities didn't know at this stage was that the robbery had been planned for some considerable time. "Businessman"

Leonardo Notarbartolo had rented an office within the diamond centre three years prior to the robbery in 2000. He had gained a reputation as a businessman while earning credibility amongst his peers. The £350-a-month office was the perfect cover for what Notarbartolo thought was the "perfect" crime. As an accredited businessman, he had 24-hour access to the building via a tenant identity card. He knew the layout of the building and the vault, located two floors beneath the centre, where he had a safe-deposit box made of steel and copper – just like those that were robbed – to add authenticity to his Italian diamond operations. As gang leader of a five-strong team, Notarbartolo bided his time at the centre until the robbery was planned, organized and set to go.

The centre itself had its own security team and was protected by a number of highly sophisticated security mechanisms, which included a lock with millions of possible combinations, infrared heat detectors and a seismic sensor. Measures also included a magnetic field and a Doppler radar; the vault should have been impenetrable. However, with his team in place, the weekend in which, of course, Notarbartolo would have unlimited access was set and the world's largest diamond heist got under way.

The loot – which not only included diamonds, but gold, gems and other jewellery – was stolen right under the noses of the centre and its security operations in what would have taken many hours. As a result, the gang had taken refreshments to the raid: it was a half-eaten sandwich that would eventually link Notarbartolo to the crime when his DNA was found at the scene. The gang, thought to be "The

School of Turin", was headed by Notarbartolo who was eventually sentenced to 10 years for his part as gang leader. In an interview after he was released on parole, the Italian claimed that the heist had been organized on behalf of a diamond merchant who hired the gang, and that it was part of an insurance fraud. He also claimed that only £20 million worth of diamonds and other jewellery were stolen.

Graff Jewellery Heist, Mayfair

(2004 and 2009)

A Pink Panther jewel thief wanted in 13 countries masterminded a £23 million raid in Britain it was revealed in 2004. Pedja Vujosevic, 29, fled with the stones on a scooter after flying in a team of thieves to help him rob Mayfair jewellers Graff in an astonishing three-minute swoop. It was Britain's biggest jewel robbery at the time and only £3 million of the haul had been found by July 2004, when the story became breaking news. Amongst the loot was a £500,000 diamond ring that was discovered in a jar of face cream belonging to one of the gang's girlfriends. The find mirrored a scene from the first Pink Panther film, starring Peter Sellers as bumbling detective Inspector Clouseau.

In July 2004, Vujosevic's sidekicks Nebojsa Denic, 34, and Milan Jovetic, 24, were sentenced at the Old Bailey for the raid. Their boss, a master of disguise known as Marco from Montenegro, was being held in France. He was suspected of raids in Europe and the Far East, including the theft of the £17 million Comtesse de Vendome necklace in Tokyo in March 2004. Detective Inspector Andy Dunn of the Flying Squad said: "He is part of a prolific East European crime syndicate. We don't know how many there are. Different people take part in each raid."

Kosovan Serb Denic travelled to London from his home in Switzerland – where he worked as a hospital cleaner – on a £50 easyJet flight just a week before the robbery. He was captured on CCTV while casing Graff with Jovetic. Later, he and Vujosevic, wearing suits and false wigs, posed as businessmen in order to get past security at the exclusive store. Once inside, Denic pulled a .357 Magnum from his waistband and forced staff to lie on the floor. Vujosevic smashed his way into display cases, grabbing 47 pieces of jewellery before calmly escaping on a Piaggio scooter. Denic was arrested after being tackled by 42-year-old security guard Simon Stearman. As the thug was wrestled to the ground he pulled the trigger on his gun. The bullet hit a woman passer-by in the face (the victim was lucky and ended up with only a bloody nose). Stearman – a Royal Navy Falklands veteran – gave chase to Denic after being alerted by radio of the heist. He said: "I pushed him against a wall and he pulled the Magnum from his waistband." The gun went off, missing Stearman by inches: "I had to take him to the floor before anyone got hurt. I was shot at by Argentine fighters but I was never trained to jump on gunmen in the street." Stearman, a dad of two, broke his elbow in the scuffle but said: "Adrenalin got me through." He was later hailed as a hero.

Jovetic, who had arranged the gang's accommodation, helped Vujosevic escape. The jar of face cream in which the diamond ring was found belonged to his girlfriend, Ana Stankovic, 26, who wanted the jewel for an engagement ring. Vujosevic was held in Paris, suspected of another robbery, along with his girlfriend, Gorani Pajic. Denic and Jovetic were convicted of conspiracy to rob. Judge Gerald Gordon said that Stearman and his colleague, Clinton Delo, showed "exceptional bravery". Denic was sentenced to 15 years for conspiracy to rob, having a firearm with intent and using a firearm to resist arrest. Jovetic, who helped Vujosevic escape, got five and a half years for assisting in the raid. The judge ordered £7,000 found at Jovetic's house to be shared by the two guards.

As for the raid itself, everything about the well-heeled gentlemen customers oozed class – right down to their silver handguns. Stepping from a chauffeur-driven Bentley Continental, the pair were ushered through the security doors of Graff jewellers in London's exclusive Sloane Street, the wide brim of a Panama hat obscuring the face of one of them from the CCTV cameras. They gained the confidence of the sales staff with their charm ... before pulling their guns and walking out with £23 million in diamond jewellery. In the gem dealers' world, it wasn't the bandits with sledgehammers and riding on motorbikes that concerned them: it was the "Pink Panthers". Like the fictional cat burglar Raffles, these gentlemen thieves blended in with the elite clientele of the jewellery trade, striking at its heart with devastating effectiveness, before vanishing. They preyed on diamond dealers' deference to their rich customers – who didn't like to be asked questions or treated with suspicion. While such crimes are rare, their value and audacity leave the police fumbling for answers, and insurance agents signing off millions in compensation.

But the robbery was to be the subject of a police summit at the end of July 2007 in a fortnight at Interpol's French headquarters. Police from across Europe met in response to "high-end" gangs of gem thieves. The Graff heist was certainly on the agenda. It was well known that robbers were as effective as ever despite tight security giving the impression that villains were being foiled in their attempts. While security in banks had tightened with better technology, the gem trade remained an industry where deals are made through word of mouth; traders cultivate relationships with clients who spend millions.

Then, a repeat robbery took place at Graff in 2009.

Smartly dressed and looking totally relaxed, two gunmen strolled into the posh London store before stealing gems worth £40 million in Britain's biggest jewel heist. The ice-cool robbers were captured on CCTV before they fired two shots and escaped in a daring daylight raid on the exclusive jewellers. Flying Squad detectives described the pair as "extremely dangerous" when they released pictures of the haul, including rings, necklaces and earrings. The worth of the loot dwarfed that taken in 2003.

The crooks struck at 4.20pm on a Thursday afternoon in August 2009 after stepping out of a hackney cab and convincingly walking past a security guard. They then drew handguns before snatching 43 pieces of jewellery in less than two minutes. Their loot also included a platinum white diamond ring and a ChronoGraff watch. The men dragged a female member of staff out of the store at gunpoint and fired a shot into the ground. They then jumped into a blue BMW parked nearby on New Bond Street, Mayfair, which smashed into a taxi on Dover Street a minute later. The robbers got out and fired a second shot, forcing passers-by to flee. They then switched to a silver Mercedes, speeding through Berkeley Square before stopping on Farm Street. Detectives believed that they abandoned the car and left Mayfair in a black people carrier, either a Ford Galaxy or VW Sharan.

Two of the getaway cars had drivers waiting behind the wheel and one theory is that the jewels were passed to a motorcyclist to exit the area quickly. Detective Chief Inspector Pam Mace said: "These men are extremely dangerous and fired at least two shots in busy London streets as they made their escape. Someone knows who these men are. They would undoubtedly have spoken about it beforehand or boasted about it afterwards." Police alerted ports and airports in case the robbers attempted to smuggle the jewels abroad.

The raiders, both in theirs 30s, spoke with London accents. One was about 6ft tall, slim, with dark hair and a side parting. His accomplice was of similar height, but stockier with short, Afro hair. Each wore a grey suit, white shirt and tie. Detectives were hoping their contacts in the underworld would tip them off about the identity of the two robbers. They believed that the brazen nature of the raid would be their downfall; the robbers had shown their faces to the store camera knowing that images would be released. And, they left two getaway cars, potentially containing fingerprints and DNA. That kind of bravado wasn't kept quiet for long and the police believed that the chances were that word was already buzzing around the criminal fraternity about who had carried out the raid. Police also believed that the pair had stolen to order, and that the robbers already had a secret buyer lined up when they robbed Graff. Experts predicted that the gems would be broken up and sold for a fraction of their value as the haul would be difficult to offload. Detective Inspector Jason Prins said: "They would be very difficult to offload. I believe there was already a market in place."

Later that month, it transpired that the two men had joked that even their own mothers wouldn't recognize them in their latex disguises. They transformed themselves after walking into a professional make-up studio and asked to be "aged" just hours before pulling off the raid. One of them had made an appointment under a false name two weeks prior to the heist and said that he would be "bringing a friend". They asked staff at the studio to turn them into men looking 30 years older, but were told that it would take longer than the two men had anticipated, so they agreed for the artists to apply liquid latex, make-up and they added scalp masks and wigs to complete the disguises at a cost of £450. No wonder then, that less than two hours later when they strolled into Graff jewellers they were unconcerned about being caught on CCTV. Detectives then examined security footage from the make-up studio and also took items for DNA analysis, including gowns, hairbrushes and the cash the robbers had paid for their transformations. They also swept the chairs for fingerprints.

Meanwhile, a £1 million reward was put up for the recovery of the gems and the arrest and prosecution of the two thieves. It was the largest reward offered since that by Securitas after the raid on its Tonbridge cash depot in 2006. Shortly after the robbery one of the gang was identified by his DNA and police then launched a hunt for his last known whereabouts. Officers had also found a burnt-out van that they suspected was a getaway vehicle; the VW Sharan was found in London and tested by forensic experts. Then, on 20th August 2009, two men were charged with the robbery. Solomun Beyene, 24, and Craig Calderwood, 24, were both accused of conspiracy to rob and a firearms offence. Both men were brought before Wimbledon Magistrates Court. At the same time, a third man remained in custody in connection with the raid, while a fourth man had been arrested the previous week but freed on bail. Beyene's lawyer claimed his client was completely innocent. Both men were due to appear at Kingston Crown Court on 1st September 2009. Another suspect, Jamal Mogg, 42, was also charged with conspiracy.

Eventually, five men were charged in connection with the robbery. Courtney Lawrence and Gregory Jones joined Solomun Beyene, Craig Calderwood and Jamal Mogg in court. They appeared via video-link from jail. All were remanded in custody at Kingston Crown Court until October 2009, with a trial expected in April 2010. Meanwhile, police were hunting others in the gang.

In April 2010, Calderwood claimed that he had been forced into the raid by accomplice Beyene after he was threatened with violence. He also claimed that the robbery – where staff were told they would be shot dead if they moved – was an inside job. Prosecutor Phillip Bennetts told jurors: "He says he committed the robbery under duress as he was in fear for his life and that of his family. He says, too, he was told the robbery was to take place with the knowledge of Graffs." Calderwood was believed to have burst into the London store with Aman Kassaye. Calderwood later wrote a letter to the manager of Graff apologizing for the raid. The note, found in his prison cell, read: "I'm truly sorry for the crime I committed. The man you are going to see in the video, that's not me." Kassaye, 24, also claimed that the robbery was an inside job; he admitted that he'd received make-up from a professional but insisted he was not the second gunman.

Martin Leggatt, the manager of Graff, was accused of taking part in the raid but told the court that it was "a fascinating conspiracy theory". He denied that the robbery took place as part of an insurance scam. The court heard that the firm, owned by billionaire Laurence Graff, lost £20 million in 2007 when its Sloane Street store was robbed by two gunmen. Other heists included a £23 million raid on the New Bond Street store in 2003 and a US$38 million loss in Tokyo in 2004. Kassaye was eventually convicted in June 2010 after being found guilty of conspiracy to rob, kidnap and possession of a firearm. Calderwood was the fifth man to be jailed for the crime. He got 21 years. The jewels, however, were not traced.

Frauds and Swindles

Victor Lustig

(Eiffel Tower Scam, 1925)

A newspaper report in April 1979 read: "The Eiffel Tower has had its head in the clouds for so long it has finally run into trouble". It needed a major facelift, expected to take place over a period of 10 years, but the company that ran the Eiffel Tower was having difficulty in raising the £17 million required to pay for it, because the company didn't *own* the tower. As a result, they threatened to drop the contract when their concession ran out at the end of 1979, unless Paris City Council, which did own the tower, agreed to be "a little less greedy". The icon was, and still is, unrivalled as a tourist attraction since it was erected for the World Fair in 1889. Millions of visitors have paid to go up it and admire the striking view. The Eiffel Tower – even in the 1970s – brought in a great deal of cash but maintenance was expensive. Repairs, routine inspection and re-coating the tower annually with 52 tons of paint cost around £1.25 million during the mid to later part of the 20th century. Salaries also took up about £1.4 million a year. On top of that, 18 per cent of gross taking and one-third of the profits had to go to Paris City Council. So, by the time the concessionaires had paid taxes and VAT they found that the operation was hardly worthwhile. The city council was unsure as to whether the threat not to renew the contract was a bluff or not. If the tower was forced to close, it was well known that the network of giant girders would quickly start to rot and experts said that the 7,500 tons of steel would fetch only £200,000 as scrap metal.

However, it wasn't the first time that the tower had faced a similar fate. After hearing that the French Government was struggling to pay for repairs to the Eiffel Tower in 1925, con man Victor Lustig decided to set up a scam to sell it to gullible scrap metal dealers. Posing as an official, he invited tenders but hinted a backhander was needed. One interested party, André Poisson, took the bait and stumped up 250,000 francs (about £700,000 today). Lustig fled with the loot.

In 1925, France was still recovering from the First World War, although Paris was booming. It was an ideal setting for a con artist like Lustig, whose idea for the tower dawned on him as he read a Parisian newspaper. He set out to develop a remarkable scheme. He employed a forger to produce fake government stationery and invited six scrap metal dealers to a confidential meeting at the Hôtel de Crillon. Lustig introduced himself as the deputy director general of the Ministry of Posts and Telegraphs. He explained that all six merchants had been selected as a result of their good reputations in the business. At this stage, the Eiffel Tower, built for the Exposition, was not meant to be permanent, so his plans to sell it for scrap metal were not totally implausible. However, Parisians would be outraged if they knew their national monument was to be brought down and scrapped, so he advised those attending the meeting that the plan was of the utmost secrecy. The plan was further enhanced in that the tower was in poor repair following the Great War and it wasn't inconceivable that the government would want to get rid of what was regarded by some as a blot on the beauty of France's capital city (the tower had been due to be disassembled in 1909 anyway).

The attendees were given a tour of the tower after arriving with Lustig in a rented limousine. Lustig's plan was to see just how gullible the men actually were. He asked each dealer to bid the following day while reminding them that the project was a "state secret". He already knew that André Poisson was the most enthusiastic of the would-be bidders and he also suspected that the Frenchman was looking for a quick entry into the upper echelons of Paris business leagues. Poisson, for his part, was completely taken with the idea, although his wife was suspicious.

In order to throw the couple off the scent, Lustig arranged a follow-up meeting with Poisson and his wife and hinted that he had a lavish lifestyle that he wanted to continue to enjoy, but that his funds were somewhat limited. He implied that he would require a payment on the quiet in order to seal the deal. Poisson was more than comfortable dealing with a corrupt "official" who wanted a bribe, and was more convinced than ever that he should proceed with the plan. He readily paid the 250,000 francs to secure the deal and a large bribe to Lustig. Laden with cash, Lustig took the train to Vienna with an accomplice. Poisson failed to follow up on the scam. Too embarrassed and humiliated, he failed to take the matter to the police or government officials. Lustig tried the scam again a month later, with a different set of dealers, but had to make a hasty escape when one of the intended victims realized what was going on and went to the police before the cash was handed over to the con artist.

John Haigh

(1944–49)

In February 1949, Scotland Yard learned that Olive Durand-Deacon, a wealthy Kensington widow who had vanished just over a week before, had secretly been associating with a man who, unknown to her, had a criminal record. The discovery, and the fact that 10 days before she had ordered dinner for the night she disappeared, ruled out the suicide theory that police first considered. Divisional Detective Inspector Sheeley Symes, in charge of the investigation, believed that the widow might have been murdered. Robbery had also been considered, as on the day she failed to return to the Onslow Court Hotel in Kensington, southwest London, she had been wearing at least £500 worth of jewellery and a Persian lamb coat. But the jewellery had failed to turn up at any jewellers or pawnbrokers.

One theory that the police were keen to pursue was that the wealthy widow had parted with money, probably as an investment, and possibly found that she had been tricked. It was possible that the victim had threatened to expose the person involved and that her life had then been in danger. Amongst those worried by her disappearance was John Haigh, a resident at the hotel where she lived, and whom she had arranged to meet at the Army and Navy store in Victoria Street. She failed to keep the appointment. John Haigh spoke to a reporter about his relationship with Mrs Durand-Deacon and what had happened on the Friday night that he last saw her. In room 404 at the Onslow Court Hotel, while leaning against the mantlepiece, he told the reporter: "I have no theories at all as to what happened. I am an inventor. I became friendly with Mrs Durand-Deacon about five years ago when she came to the hotel. She was very fussy about her appearance. She had no fingernails at all and used to make artificial ones out of coloured paper." He went on to describe how the widow knew he was an inventor and she had asked him to make artificial fingernails for her so she had agreed to provide the 40-year-old with a sample. Haigh claimed that he'd waited outside the store for an hour before driving down to his factory in Crawley, Sussex, when she didn't keep the appointment. Haigh was then questioned three times about the woman's disappearance, after he went to the police with another resident from the hotel to report Mrs Durand-Deacon missing. He said: "I know everyone is linking my name with hers, I can't help that."

In March 1949, Scotland Yard detectives carried out experiments on a car in an effort to clear up the mystery of the missing wealthy London widow. They made test runs from the centre of London to a spot within a 30-mile radius in order to check the time it would have taken Mrs Durand-Deacon if she had travelled out of the capital on the day she disappeared. The tests were organized following a Scotland Yard conference of senior officers at which a map of London and the Home Counties area was studied by Symes and his team. A "corridor" stretching from London towards Eastbourne was marked out and police in the areas were asked to search woods and ponds.

Later that same month, press reports confirmed that the man believed to have murdered Mrs Durand-Deacon, 69, might have killed several other rich widows. The information came to light just a few hours after what were believed to be the remains of Mrs Durand-Deacon were found in a factory yard in Crawley. After the victim was murdered, it was believed that her body was immersed in a "cremation bath" of sulphuric acid. An oil-fed bonfire under an elderberry tree made a pyre for what little of the body had not been eaten away by the acid.

Senior detectives making inquiries into the case gave special attention to reports on other elderly widows who had also disappeared in the years just before and just after the Second World War. The women thought to have been murdered had all lived in hotels and had money to invest in quick-return ventures. Police also checked the files on girls who had gone missing within the previous two years. Scotland Yard detectives were convinced that the murderer was a fraudster or swindler with a split personality and who was efficient at attracting elderly widows. Police were also convinced that they knew who this man was. He was reported to have been living in luxury, although he had served fairly lengthy jail terms for fraud and theft.

There were, however, only a few clues to help in identifying the murder victim discovered at the factory, which had been deserted for at least a month. With regard to the body, only residue of tissue was found by the Home Office pathologist Dr Keith Simpson, who had scoured the area along with officers from Scotland Yard and Sussex CID. There were, however, charred rims of a pair of glasses, part of a red plastic handbag (exactly like the one used by Olive Durand-Deacon), parts of a watch and some metal beads. In a shed at the factory, used as a storeroom for a local engineering firm, there was an empty sulphuric acid container; the 30-gallon oil drum believed to have been used as a "bath" stood in the yard.

All the items were taken to the police laboratories at Hendon for examination, as were numbered boxes of sweepings from the shed floor, a white shoebox, four brown-paper parcels and boxes of earth. Dr Simpson was given samples of earth, ashes, mud and oily substances in order to build a "picture" of the murdered victim. The Persian lamb coat, worn by the victim on the day she went missing, was eventually found at a dry-cleaners in Surrey. Detective Inspector Symes and Superintendent Tom Barratt, alongside Chief Inspector Mahon – who were all investigating the murder – were confident of making an arrest fairly quickly. They held a meeting shortly before midnight on 1st March 1949 while John Haigh, who was already at the station, remained there. His story about Olive Durand-Deacon failing to turn up outside the Army and Navy store obviously just wasn't convincing enough.

By 2nd April 1949, John George Haigh sat in the dock accused of murder. A 35-minute opening address was given by the prosecutor, Robey, at Horsham Magistrates Court in Sussex, which ended with: "The case the Crown presents here today is the case that this man committed a carefully planned murder for gain." During the trial, the court would hear how Haigh had allegedly told police that: "Mrs Durand-Deacon no longer exists. She has disappeared completely, and no trace of her will ever be found again." Asked what had happened to her, Haigh was alleged to have said: "I have destroyed her in acid. Every trace has gone. How can you prove murder if there is no body?"

But Robey declared to the court in dramatic fashion that the accused "was wrong".

He described the human remains found in sludge outside the Crawley storeroom in which Haigh was alleged to have shot the woman on 18th February before dissolving her body in sulphuric acid. Haigh calmly met the gaze of a number of witnesses called into court to identify him. He met their searching stares levelly, inclined his head slightly and smiled. He occasionally put on a pair of glasses in order to look at documents and notes. For the most part, Haigh sat between his escorts with folded arms and closed eyes. The court heard how Haigh's dining table in the hotel restaurant was close to that of the elderly widow's and that, unsurprisingly, the two became fairly friendly. Haigh, an engineer, was a nominal director of Hurstlea Products, a light-engineering firm who kept its storeroom in Leopold Road, Crawley. He used it for experimental work. As a man who gambled on horses and dogs, he had made some substantial gains. However, he had also suffered substantial losses and was known to have had an unsecured overdraft of £83. 5s. 10d. on 7th February 1949. At that time, he also owed the Onslow Court Hotel around £50 for board and lodging and was under pressure to pay. Robey argued that the financial situation of the suspect was crucial in the case against him. On 15th February, Haigh had borrowed money from his firm's managing director, Jones, who advised Haigh that he would have to repay the money no later than 20th February. Haigh had told Jones that he was bringing someone to Crawley who was interested in the manufacture of artificial fingernails and had suggested that they could be made of some plastic materials or Cellophane.

After his arrest, a shopping list in Haigh's handwriting was found in his hotel room, which included the name of a company that supplied large oil drums. Also on the list were a drum of sulphuric acid, a stirrup pump, gloves, apron, cotton wool pad and some red paper. With the loan from Jones, he had paid off the hotel, but needed the funds to pay back his creditor. On 17th February, Haigh went to Blagdens Wharf in London and bought a large green drum with a corrosive inside. He then travelled to Crawley, taking with him a new stirrup pump. He asked Jones to remove the leg of the pump, getting him to knock out the rivets. The reason for this, the prosecution argued, was so that there was room for the stirrup pump in the container.

Having previously claimed that he drove to Crawley without the victim, Haigh had, during questioning, said that he drove Olive Durand-Deacon to the factory at about 2.30pm on the afternoon in question. He had taken her into the George Hotel, Crawley for a few minutes and they were spotted driving away in his car. The victim was then taken to the storeroom, where she was shot in the back of the head while examining some paper; red Cellophane paper had been found at the scene. After removing the victim's coat and jewellery and taking 30 shillings from her red handbag, he then dumped her body into the drum, together with the handbag and the rest of its contents that were of no use to him. He then went to see Jones and claimed that the person with whom he had a meeting had failed to show up. Haigh was spotted back at the factory by a van driver and then again in a restaurant at about 7.00pm that night, where he had a pot of tea.

Haigh then admitted returning to the store and pumping acid into the drum using the stirrup pump. At 9.00pm he went to the George Hotel, Crawley for dinner. He returned to London on 19th February. Here he spoke to Mrs Lane – another resident at the hotel – and told her that Olive had failed to meet him the day before as arranged. He then drove to Putney, where he sold the victim's gold and ruby watch-bracelet for £10. Using the name F Miller at the jewellers, he gave a false address and then returned to Crawley to see what was happening in the drum. He decided that the acid hadn't worked as quickly as it could, so he left the body and took away the coat.

Haigh then went to Horsham and visited a jewellers, where he asked if they could value some jewellery for probate. He was advised to return on Monday when someone would be able to help him. It was on the Monday that he and Mrs Lane went to the police to report Olive missing. Haigh decided on 22nd February that the destruction of the body was complete (although it wasn't) and he emptied the drum completely and left it in the yard. He accepted £100 from the jewellers in Horsham for the remainder of the jewellery and he then paid Jones the money he had borrowed; it was two days late. He had disposed of the victim's chain and keys in the ground at Buxted, but these were later recovered, along with a gun and bullets that were found at the storeroom. During the trial, Lily Patricia Mayo, a dental surgeon, confirmed that she had made false teeth for the victim when she was shown them in court, while Olive's sister, Esme Fargus, identified her jewellery. Mrs Lane identified the victim's red handbag. There were 27 witnesses and six police officers called to give evidence against Haigh.

In July 1949, as the trial continued, it was alleged that John Haigh (on trial at Lewes Assizes) had confessed to murdering nine people over a period of five years. He had allegedly drunk their blood and then destroyed their bodies in acid. The victims included Mr and Mrs Donald McSwann and their son, Donald; Dr and Mrs Archibald Henderson; and two women and a man whom he could not identify. At first he pleaded not guilty to the murder of Olive Durand-Deacon. Later, however, his counsel, Sir David Maxwell Fyfe, told a hushed court that he would ask for "a special verdict – guilty of the acts charged, but insane at the time they were committed". Haigh claimed that he was "in some mystic way controlled by a guiding spirit". His counsel argued that: "When the opportunity came to do these dreadful deeds, he felt that he was carrying out not his own desires, but the divinely appointed course which had been set for him." His counsel went on to describe how Haigh, who had been brought up in extremely severe surroundings, had been living in a life of dreams. However, the prosecution, led by Sir Hartley Shawcross, argued that the murder of Olive Durand-Deacon had been carefully premeditated for gain. Haigh had admitted to drawing blood from the victim's neck and then drinking it. He also admitted to police that in 1944 he disposed of William (Donald) McSwann in a similar manner and then, in 1946, the victim's parents, Donald and Amy, at 79 Gloucester Road, London. He then chose a woman from Hammersmith and killed her in the same way. He had killed the Hendersons for around £300 and another man who he met at a pub in High Street Kensington. It was alleged by the prosecution that all the murders were carried out "for gain".

Haigh was convicted of the murder of Olive Durand-Deacon on 19th July 1949. It had been one of the most shocking dramas in the history of British criminal courts and, in just two days, the court had gone through the whole "amazing" story of confessions to nine murders, the drinking of blood, and the strange dreams of an ex-choirboy who believed he was controlled by a divine and mystic force. It took the jury of 11 men and one woman just 13 minutes to reject the insanity plea: they agreed with the prosecution that the man in the dock was "bad" not "mad". Despite the drama in the courtroom, which continued to the end of the trial, the only person who seemed unaffected by proceedings was the accused himself. He remained aloof and disinterested; a man playing a leading, yet silent role. He lounged in the dock while the battle to save him from the gallows raged on around him. When the jury brought in their verdict, he stood to attention and said he had nothing to say to the guilty verdict. Two thousand people, mainly women, turned up outside the court to applaud the verdict. Haigh was driven away to the death cell at Wandsworth Prison. He was hanged for murder in August 1949. Just hours later, a new effigy was added to the Chamber of Horrors at Madame Tussauds waxworks in London, where visitors were invited to gape at the murderer of nine innocent victims. In September 1949, it was announced that Olive Durand-Deacon had left a will of £36,808, with an annuity of £250, to go to Dame Christabel Pankhurst, the daughter of Emmeline Pankhurst, who had stepped up as suffragette leader following her mother's death in 1928.

Dr John Bodkin Adams

(1956)

Detective Superintendent Herbert Hannam of Scotland Yard's murder squad was called as a surprise witness into the inquest of the death of Gertrude Joyce Hullett, 50, on 21st August 1956. A crowded court in Eastbourne was silent as Hannam was asked by the coroner, Dr A C Sommerville, if Scotland Yard had been asked to help in investigating certain deaths in the Sussex neighbourhood. "Yes, sir", came the detective's reply. The jury then returned a verdict that Mrs Hullett, a wealthy widow, had committed suicide by an overdose of barbiturate drugs. They had heard how her doctor, Dr John Bodkin Adams, claimed she was depressed. They heard him say how she had talked of suicide. Meanwhile, Hannam was to start an investigation into the deaths of more than 12 elderly and wealthy women.

Hannam had been in court for the five-hour inquest on Hullett, who inherited £84,000 when her second husband died in March 1956. The coroner said that she had complained of a headache and went to bed at 10.00pm on 19th July that same year. She was found – apparently asleep – the next morning, but later that day was obviously unconscious. She remained unconscious until she died on 23rd July. Her body contained 112 grains of barbiturates. Mrs Hullett's daughter, Evelyn Tomlinson, had told the inquest that her mother had been unhappy since the death of her husband and that she had said she did not want to live. The victim had been taking sleeping tablets, prescribed by her doctor, John Bodkin Adams. Hullett had had complete faith in her physician but, in November 1956, Adams was facing 13 offences when it was alleged that he forged documents, used false pretences and falsity in procuring cremations.

The 57-year-old had been arrested at his house in Trinity Trees, Eastbourne earlier in the month by Hannam, who had just completed a seven-week investigation. The arrest followed a series of meetings in London between Scotland Yard chiefs and the Director of Public Prosecutions, Sir Theobald Mathew. Adams was charged and then released on £100 bail.

Adams had been practicing for 34 years when he was remanded on £2,000 bail at Eastbourne Magistrates Court on 26th November 1956. Of the 13 charges brought against him, four were brought under the Cremation Act. Further charges alleged the forging of prescriptions. He was remanded until 20th December and required to surrender his passport. He was then charged with the murder of a wealthy 81-year-old widow, Edith Morrell, who had died at her mansion home in 1950. Her estate had amounted to more than £77,000. Adams appeared before magistrates on 20th December 1956 in connection with the murder and the 13 other charges under the Cremation Act, the Forgery Act and the Larceny Act. The Irish-born, portly doctor also faced three additional charges, including attempting to conceal two bottles of morphine on 24th November 1956, on the same day that he did "wilfully obstruct" a police officer in the exercise of his powers and that (also on the same day) he failed to comply with the Dangerous

Drugs Regulations on keeping a record.

It was decided between the prosecution and the defence counsel that the additional 16 charges would be looked into once the murder charge had been dealt with. The full hearing was expected to begin on 14th January 1957 lasting four days. Three hours after the December court hearing, Adams was driven to Brixton Prison in London. When the case came to trial in January, there was a sensational allegation that the doctor had murdered three people, although he appeared on only one charge of murder: that he poisoned Edith Morrell. For more than two hours, defending counsel argued that certain evidence that the prosecution intended to call should be heard in closed court. The magistrates closed the court to the public so that they could consider the submission and then ruled that the full prosecution case should be heard in public. The deaths of two other patients of Adams were extremely similar to that of Mrs Morrell, and the court decided that it was essential that the facts surrounding their deaths should be given in evidence in connection with the murder charge. The two victims were named as Alfred Hullett and his wife Gertrude. The prosecutor, Melford Stevenson, alleged that Mr Hullett died from an overdose of morphia injected by Adams. He was seen by a nurse taking the morphia from his case in a "darkened corner of the bedroom". Under Hullett's last will, Adams had received £500; the doctor had stated that he thought he would have been left more. Adams was then alleged to have poisoned Mrs Hullett with barbiturates. Six days before her death, she had given the doctor a cheque for £1,000. He had presented the cheque to his bank and had asked for it to be "specially cleared". Counsel then explained to the court that a bank would stop a cheque if the person on whose account it was to be drawn dies. The prosecution argued that Adams had known Mrs Hullett would die because he planned to murder her. Adams was also alleged to have injected massive quantities of drugs into Mrs Morrell. For this reason, Morrell had become a drug addict, dependent on the doctor for the supplies that she craved. She altered her will and bequeathed a Rolls-Royce and a chest of Georgian silver to her doctor. The prosecution then alleged that the victim died four months later because the doctor stepped up the drug dosage. The prosecution alleged that the doctor's motive was pure and simple: greed.

On 14th January 1957, four nurses who gave an elderly widow drug injections on the instructions of Adams told the court about the times that the doctor injected the widow himself without revealing to them what the drugs were. Caroline Randall spoke about the two "bigger than usual" doses that were given to Edith Morrell shortly before she died. The nurse said that she herself had injected the drug at the doctor's request with a syringe he had prepared. She added that the doctor had not told her what the drug was. Another nurse, Brenda Hughes, described the night before Mrs Morrell died. She said that Adams arrived at about 10.00pm and prepared an injection of around 5cc. She had noted that she thought the syringe held a rather large dose and came from the doctor's bag.

Next came evidence about the cremations of Morrell and the Hullett couple by Dr Herbert Walker, medical referee at Downs Crematorium in Brighton. He said that a cremation form relating to Morrell was signed by John B Adams, while cause of death was given as cerebral thrombosis; Dr Walker duly signed the authority for cremation. Adams had also signed the form for Alfred Hullett and cause of death was given as cerebral haemorrhage. Adams had uttered the cause of death for the victim without even looking at the body, said nurse Gladys Miller, while giving evidence about the last hours of life of Mr Hullett. She also described how she had tried to turn the light on as Adams had administered an injection to Hullett, but that the doctor had told her not to bother. The nurse was convinced that the bottle taken from his bag contained morphia; Miller stated how another bottle she had seen – just like the one in the bedroom that night – contained hyperduric morphia. Within five minutes of the injection the patient lay asleep but his breathing was particularly heavy, recalled the nurse. He died at 6.30am the following morning. When Adams was called back to the Hullett's home following the death, he cited the cause of death as cerebral haemorrhage before he even looked at the body of Alfred Hullett.

Two other doctors were also called to give evidence against Adams, including Arthur Shera and Peter Cook, as was Kenneth Pill, the cashier at Midland Bank who had dealt with the cheque given to Adams by Mrs Hullett. In court, when questioned by the prosecution, a further witness, Angus Sommerville, stated that he had received a phone call from Adams the day before Mrs Hullett died, asking for a private post-mortem. When asked by Sommerville what Mrs Hullett had died from, Adams told the coroner that she wasn't yet dead. He was denied a private post-mortem by the coroner and asked to follow the proper channels once there was actually a death to report.

The next witness was a Scotland Yard scientist, Michael Moss, who told the magistrates court that the test he made on drugs prescribed by Adams were, in actual fact, double the strength that they indicated on the bottles. Moss was the last witness to be called to the trial. He gave full testimony about the tests he had carried out on three bottles and was also questioned about a post-mortem examination he made on Mrs Hullett. He confirmed that: "The quantity of barbitone is in excess of the minimum recorded fatal dose." In February 1957 the court decided that Adams should stand trial for the murder of Edith Morrell at the Old Bailey. The nine-day hearing had helped magistrates decide that he would stand trial, despite a dramatic plea from his defending counsel that the doctor should be discharged. Thirty minutes after the hearing concluded, Adams was driven to Brixton Prison to await his fate.

When the trial began at the Old Bailey on 18th March 1957, the opening arguments concentrated on the words used by Adams when he was arrested for the murder of Edith Morrell. He had said to police: "Murder, can you prove it was murder? I did not think you could prove murder." Would these have been the words of an innocent man? Or, were they the words of a murderer who really didn't think he could be caught, argued Sir Reginald Manningham-Buller, QC. Sir Reginald faced the jury and added: "I submit to you that the evidence will prove, and prove conclusively, this old lady was murdered by Dr Adams." But Adams maintained his innocence and told the court: "I am not guilty, my lord." Sir Reginald then opened the case for the Crown and told the jury of Dr Adam's qualifications as a Doctor of Medicine and a Bachelor of Surgery, and that he held diplomas in public health and anaesthetics. He argued that Adams was not ignorant of the effects of drugs and, in particular, the effect of morphia and heroin. Edith Morrell, despite not being in pain following a stroke, was routinely given large quantities of barbiturates, morphia and heroin by Adams. The victim had, in fact, become addicted to the drugs she was being prescribed and had both a craving and a dependence on them.

Adams, who was the source of the supply, had telephoned Morrell's solicitor, Hubert Sogno, on 28th April 1949 to explain that his patient was extremely anxious about the contents of her will and that she wanted to see her solicitor that day. The court heard how Mrs Morrell had altered her will previously, but had never made any bequest to Dr Adams. Mr Sogno did visit his client who then made a new will dated 9th June 1949, in which she bequeathed to Adams an oak chest containing silver. Adams called on Sogno on 8th March 1950 (without an appointment) and told the solicitor that Morrell had also promised him her Rolls-Royce but she had forgotten to include it in the latest will. As a result, a codicil to the will was added; Sogno told the court that the proposed gifts to the doctor were of considerable value. Adams told Sogno that the codicil should be executed immediately, but later destroyed if Mrs Morrell's son did not like the new bequests. It seemed quite an extraordinary demand on the part of the doctor. Mrs Morrell also left the doctor her house and all her personal chattels should her son die before her.

In his summing up of the case, Justice Devlin said that if Adams

– as the prosecution alleged – was "angling for a legacy" from Edith Morrell, and deliberately gave her drugs to get her under his influence, then it was not a pretty story. The summing up, which lasted three hours, came after 16 days of trial in the Crown case against Adams. The 10 men and two women on the jury found him not guilty on 9th April 1957 and Adams stumbled from the dock of the Old Bailey with tears running down his cheeks. He had been found not guilty of murder, and a further indictment accusing him of the murder of Mrs Hullett was also dropped. He was driven away from court to a secret hideaway, where he had time to recover from the trial before being back in court – on 15 further charges – on 20th May 1957. On 26th July, he was eventually fined £2,400 at Lewes Assizes for offences under the Forgery, Cremation and Dangerous Drugs Acts; his legacies had brought him £30,000 in 10 years. He admitted to 14 charges during the four-day hearing and was struck off the medical register on 27th November that same year. He made two failed attempts to get back on the register before being reinstated as a general practitioner on 22nd November 1961. When Adams died in 1983, it came to light that the doctor had been a fairly wealthy man. At the time of his death, his estate was estimated to be around £250,000.

Guinness Share-trading Fraud

(1986)

What happened at Guinness in 1986? The inspectors carried out a probe to examine circumstances suggesting the misconduct of the affairs of Guinness in connection with its membership (shareholders). They looked into the affairs of the company, especially at certain interests in its shares. Why? Because there were strong rumours that Guinness shares were caught up in "insider trading" during its bitter £2,500 million battle with Argyll, the Presto supermarket chain, for the takeover of the drinks company Distillers earlier in 1986. The claim that the company was using insider trading involved using secret information to make a fast buck on share deals. Obviously, some workers and managers in banks or financial groups will be "in the know" about certain big deals that will be taking place, but it is illegal to cash in on this knowledge – even by tipping off someone outside the company to buy shares.

In the case of suspicions at Guinness, under the Companies Act and the new Financial Service Act (which came into force in November 1986), Department of Trade (DoT) inspectors decided to look into the company's affairs – and it would have been illegal for any member of staff to refuse to give information to the investigation under oath. The City had already been hit by a number of high-profile scandals in previous years and, prior to the Guinness enquiry, there had been quite a fight for the City to show that it could keep its own business in order without outside interference. Revelations by the disgraced US financier Ivan Boesky rocked the City and led to strong rumours linking Guinness with insider share deals during the takeover battle with Distillers.

As a result of the goings on, on 30th December 1986 top City bankers Morgan Grenfell quit as advisers to Guinness, who were by then under investigation by the Board of Trade. One of the bank's high-flying directors, Roger Seelig, resigned his £200,000-a-year job, while the firm stressed that his resignation was not related to share dealings on his own account. Seelig was a key part of helping Guinness to win its £2,500 million takeover of Distillers in the Spring of 1986 and, during the battle, Guinness shares worth £6 million were bought and resold to an unknown buyer. The deal pushed up the price of the company's shares and helped clinch the takeover. Morgan Grenfell said that the bank quit because their relationship with Guinness had become strained. The news came as a bitter blow to the brewing giant. Next came the shock announcement that Guinness chief Ernest Saunders had dramatically stepped down as boss of the troubled drinks giant following a government inquiry into the company.

Saunders resigned at the beginning of January 1987 stating: "I feel personally that because of the uncertainty and disruption that has been caused to the business as a result of the inquiry, my action would be in the best interest of the company, its shareholders, employees and my family. It is my personal view that it is of paramount importance that this fine company's progress should be allowed to proceed as planned and that the action I am taking should enable this to be achieved." Saunders had joined the company in 1981 when it was a "sleepy giant" going nowhere and shares were worth about 50p each. In just five years, he had turned it into one of the most successful drinks companies in the world, with shares rising to £3.50.

Following a three-hour board meeting in mid-January, two other members of staff were asked to step down, too. These included Swiss banker Dr Arthur Furer, who had once been Saunders' boss at Nestlé, and American lawyer Thomas Ward. The board also discussed allegations of secret £200 million share dealing during the takeovers of Johnnie Walker and Gordon's gin. Finance Director Olivier Roux had left the company that same week and it seemed that the whole of Saunders' regime had been swept aside by the board. Meanwhile, the gigantic scandal about the company and its share dealings rocked the stock exchange, and there were signs that the debacle could shake up the rules governing takeover bids. But what, exactly, had gone wrong at Guinness?

The company was accused of secretly setting up (with the help of bankers) £200 million worth of share deals in London, Zurich, New York and Vienna. This was because both Guinness and Distillers – as international companies – had friends, contacts and shareholders in the world's main money centres and a Zurich bank said that its business relationship with the company was subject to "Swiss banking secrecy laws". There was also the question of Ivan Boesky's involvement. The disgraced American was fined £70 million in 1986 for making an illegal fortune gained by inside information about companies. He was then alleged to have bought big blocks of both Guinness and Distillers shares during the takeover battle, which led to Guinness secretly investing US$100 million in a Boesky fund after their victory in the takeover in May 1986.

Guinness admitted to the unlawful share deals on 16th January 1987, just 10 days after Saunders' departure. Its shares then crashed by £150 million. The secret deals had been made through a Swiss bank – as suspected – and the disclosure came from new chairman Sir Norman Macfarlane, who also confirmed that a pile of bills amounting to £25 million had been found at the company. The invoices were thought to be fees paid to third parties for "advice and services" believed to be connected with the takeover bid. In a letter to shareholders, Sir Norman said: "As yet, no satisfactory explanation has been provided for these invoices." Guinness directors were worried that they might have involved payments for people who had bought shares to help Guinness win control of Distillers. Sir Norman revealed that Guinness had put £50 million into the Luxembourg offshoot of a Swiss bank in connection with share deals that were "in apparent breach of the Companies Act".

Sir Norman said that Bank Leu of Switzerland had bought a lot of shares on the strength of an agreement that "Guinness could not lawfully have fulfilled". He stated that an agreement to buy back the shares later had been signed by two Guinness directors, Olivier Roux and Thomas Ward. Guinness shareholders were also advised that dividends worth £55 million, which they had been expecting later in January 1987, were unlikely to be paid until legal and accounting matters were cleared up. A further blow to the shares came when Argyll, which lost out in the takeover bid, were considering legal action against the drinks company. Michael Howard, the then corporate affairs minister, assured MPs in the Commons that there was no question of keeping anything about the Guinness inquiry under wraps.

Just a few days later, millionaire tycoon Gerald Ronson admitted that he had secretly accepted money from Guinness. He stated that Guinness had paid his company £5.8 million to help them in the takeover battle and that the money was used to buy and boost the value of shares. Ronson, who was deeply embarrassed, sent the money back to Guinness in January 1987 and said: "I am very upset to have been involved, even in good faith." But, that meant that another £19 million was still unaccounted for and it was suspected that more top City figures would be dragged into what had turned out to be the biggest scandal in the Square Mile since the Second World War.

The scandal certainly rocked the world of high finance, despite a long history of City swindlers and even though, according to reports at the time, Guinness hadn't actually done anything that was as bad as some other scandals. However, what was once quite legal and common practice in the City had been outlawed in the latest Companies Act. It was, by this time, illegal for any company to buy its own shares – except in special circumstances – or to get other people to buy them with a promise that they wouldn't lose out in doing so. The scandal came at a time when millions of small investors had been buying shares for the first time, with government encouragement.

At the end of January 1987, supermarket tycoon Jimmy Gulliver swooped on scandal-hit Guinness with an offer to take over the company. He had lost millions when the drinks giant had beaten his Argyll company in the dirty takeover battle for Distillers, and Gulliver had already threatened to sue for vast damages. But, Sir Norman was unconvinced by the letter he received from Gulliver and said that he saw no benefit from talking to the tycoon about a "friendly merger". Meanwhile, top commodity dealers Berisford admitted that it had bought £1.5 million worth of shares and that it planned to send the money – taken by one of its offshoots – back to the disgraced Guinness; and Lord Spens, a director of Ansbacher, quit his job, thus becoming the eighth victim of the Guinness row.

As the investigation continued, it came to light that City stockbroker Tony Parnes had been paid £3 million for his "key advice" in the bitter takeover. Parnes claimed that the fee "reflected the true value of his services", but denied that any of the £3 million went towards propping up the price of shares. By April 1987, it transpired that Saunders had secretly arranged for £3 million to go to his Swiss bank account. The high court heard how during the takeover £5.2 million was paid for "services rendered" to a Jersey company owned by Guinness director Thomas Ward. Then, £3 million was transferred to Saunders' account. Saunders denied the allegations of fraud and breach of trust and denied making money out of the takeover.

At the hearing, it was also announced that both Saunders and Ward were seeking removal of an injunction granted to Guinness, freezing £5.2 million of their assets in Britain. The next evidence in the scandal came when Guinness suffered a riddle over £82 million when

Saunders claimed that the total expenses of the takeover were around £182 million (former finance chief Olivier Roux had told shareholders that the figure was £100 million). Saunders then denied at the hearing that he had ordered the destruction of key papers in the battle. He said that claims by his former secretary that he had them shredded were "completely untrue". However, former secretary Margaret McGrath claimed in April 1987 that she had destroyed three diaries with "great reluctance". She also claimed that Saunders had been unusually insistent that the diaries should be destroyed. The court then ruled, later that month, that the £5.2 million payment from Saunders to Ward for his services during the takeover was unlawful. The judge ruled that as the two men had failed to disclose their interest to the Guinness board the agreement could not have been lawfully made. He also rejected the two men's bid to lift injunctions freezing their assets and said that Saunders – who was then living in Switzerland – would probably move his assets out of Britain. Ward was ordered to pay what was left of the £5.2 million into a special account pending the outcome of the dispute.

But things went from bad to worse for the former Guinness boss when millionaire businessman Tiny Rowland put up £250,000 bail in May 1987 to keep Saunders out of jail. Herbert Heinzel guaranteed a further £250,000 at Bow Street Magistrates Court, where Saunders was accused of perverting the course of justice, and destroying and falsifying documents. His passport was retained by police and he wasn't allowed to apply for any travel documents or to contact any past or present employees of Guinness. After his release, Saunders warned: "Those responsible for my present situation will be exposed. I am incensed at the allegations of dishonesty and wrongdoing made against me. All the charges are strenuously denied and will be vigorously contested." He then resigned from the Guinness board, just hours before fellow board members were asked to "kick" him off the board at the AGM. Until this time, he had refused to resign as a director despite being fired from his top job some months earlier. Saunders claimed that he had played no part in and had no knowledge of any unlawful transaction; he also denied benefitting in any way from the £25 million that former directors allegedly paid out improperly to people who bought shares.

In October 1987, Ronson was back in the headlines when he was accused of stealing more than £6 million. He was the second friend of the then prime minister, Margaret Thatcher, to be charged within a week over the scandal. He was to appear before Bow Street Magistrates Court on eight charges. He had been arrested after he went voluntarily to Fraud Squad headquarters on 13th October. Ronson was the fourth top City man held over the £2.8 billion takeover. By this time, Saunders was facing a further 37 charges, including theft of nearly £24 million. Sir Jack Lyons, also a friend of Thatcher, had been charged with nine offences in connection with the Guinness probe, while Tony Parnes was arrested in America.

In June 1988, Saunders represented himself in court when he was refused legal aid for a solicitor. Said to be financially ruined, Saunders was living on a monthly allowance – while his assets were frozen – and had 25 files served against him by the Serious Fraud Office. In

July that year, he asked the court to end the "inhuman" ordeal and to conduct a speedy hearing of the 40 charges he faced. His request was denied by the court. He also failed in 1990 to have reporting restrictions imposed on the first of two trials arising from the Guinness affair. He was the only one of the seven accused to face charges in both trials and he feared that the second jury would be prejudiced by what they would read of the first.

In February 1990, the court heard how Saunders was "greedy" when he masterminded a plan to win the takeover battle for the giant Distillers group. At the opening of the trial, prosecutor John Chadwick, QC, told the jury they would not need special knowledge or expertise of the City to decide the real issues. He continued that Saunders had tried to find people to buy up lots of Guinness shares. Parnes and Lyons were recruited to the alleged scam and Ronson's company received more than £5 million for its help. Chadwick said: "Parnes, Lyons and Ronson, with the approval of Saunders, sent invoices to Guinness that were dishonest. It was done so they could be paid huge sums of money for their help in the unlawful shares operation. Those parties were so carried away by greed and ambition that they were prepared to break the law."

On 27th August 1990, Saunders, Ronson, Parnes and Lyons were all convicted. The 112-day trial was said to have cost up to £30 million. The defence cost about £7 million; the prosecution £4 million. There was the cost of putting the men in the dock (estimated at £1.6 million) and the massive expense of running the court. On 28th August 1990 Saunders received a five-year jail sentence. Parnes was given two and a half years, while Ronson received one year and a £5 million fine. Lyons, who was out on bail pending an operation, was due to be sentenced in September.

The three men jailed then sparked controversy when they were moved to a "soft" open prison two days after being sentenced. They were moved to the Ford Prison in Sussex, where all three demanded single rooms, and warders even carried the men's bags. Meanwhile, Olivier Roux, who helped convict the three men, denied that he was given immunity from prosecution by stating: "I made no deal." On 25th September 1990, Lyons was fined £3 million but escaped being sent to jail due to the fact that the court was told he had cancer, a weak heart and high blood pressure. He could, if healthy, have expected a three-year sentence, but four doctors advised that time behind bars could kill the crooked millionaire.

Saunders' lawyers told the London Appeal Court in April 1991 that he was suffering from an incurable depressive illness. A neurologist said that the 55-year-old did not know who was the president of the United States at the start of the Gulf War. Eventually, in May 1991, his jail term was halved when appeal judges ruled that his prison term was "substantially too high". He was released on parole on 28th June 1991, 20 months before the end of his sentence. Just three years later, Saunders was hoping to be in line for a multi-million pound compensation award after his fraud conviction was sensationally referred to the Appeal Court in December 1994. New evidence had come to light and, in a dramatic turnaround, the government came under intense pressure to disband the Serious Fraud Office (SFO) after the fiasco over the Guinness case. The Labour Party said that the SFO had become an embarrassment. Lord Spens, who was cleared of fraud in a separate Guinness trial, angrily dismissed the SFO as "inherently and fatally flawed".

In December 1995, Guinness was once again in the press when a reporter discussed the former company directors – whose appeal against conviction was thrown out by the Court of Appeal that month. Guinness must be very good for you, he mocked: Lyons had been spared jail because he was so gravely ill; Saunders was said to have an irreversible condition of pre-senile dementia and was released early. However, as soon as he was freed, it transpired that he had no such disease and was successfully running another company within months while also enjoying a skiing holiday. In fact, so incensed was the reporter who wrote the article that he stated: "I can diagnose three painfully obvious medical conditions: bare-faced cheek, sheer nerve, and a massive overproduction of gall."

Robert Maxwell and the Missing Millions

(1991)

The body of Robert Maxwell, publishing giant, was found in the Atlantic Ocean on 5th November 1991. The 68-year-old Mirror Group publisher was discovered off the Canary Islands after disappearing from his yacht during a holiday cruise. The death of Maxwell, who created a global publishing empire and counted world leaders among his friends, stunned heads of big business and politics. His last hours were shrouded in mystery. He'd last been seen strolling on deck at 4.25am. He made a phone call 20 minutes later, then he simply vanished. His son, Philip Maxwell, had flown to Tenerife with his mother, Betty Maxwell, as soon as the publisher went missing and, later, they formally identified his body in Las Palmas. Maxwell, the only passenger on board the yacht, had joined the 180ft *Lady Ghislaine* – named after his daughter – in Gibraltar for a few days' rest. The sea was calm and weather conditions were good; no one could understand how Maxwell had ended up overboard.

He had been a giant in every way. "A man of power which he wielded ruthlessly, and a man of kindness, which he distributed generously" was how the *Mirror* described the 250lbs man, whose physical presence was enormous and made him appear taller than he actually was. In the days following his death, the *Mirror* wrote: "Love him or hate him, his like will not be seen again." Maxwell's greatest prize had come in 1984 when he bought Mirror Group Newspapers from its then owners, Reed International. When asked once what he wanted to be remembered for, he said: "Saving the *Daily Mirror*."

Staff at the time feared for the newspaper's future; in 1984, owning a newspaper was like pouring liquid gold down a sewer. They all lost money, or made so little that there was none left for new investment. After a strike that increased the threat even more, Maxwell instituted a survival plan that reduced the number of employees from more than 7,000 to less than 3,000. It was a devastating time for employees, but it worked. A newspaper group that was losing money in 1984, just six years later made profits before tax of more than £80 million. The money that Maxwell saved by scrapping inefficient and restrictive practices was spent on making the *Mirror* the most up-to-date national newspaper in the country and the first to publish in full colour.

His impact on the newspaper and its staff was dramatic. He was a communications enthusiast: fax machines were brought in and the obsolete practices of generations of newspaper personnel were scrapped for new technologies. He worked every waking hour and expected his senior executives to do the same. Maxwell was always available, whatever the time of day or night, and he expected his editors, directors and leader writers to follow suit. One journalist said of him: "He encouraged his executives to speak out. No one was ever sacked for being blunt, though many were fired for being evasive. There are those who started off hating him and ended up loving him, or at least standing in awe."

Maxwell was laid to rest in Jerusalem in November 1991 after a day-long autopsy revealed that he had died of respiratory cardiac arrest. But, while in Jerusalem, samples from the body were taken by pathologist Dr Iain West in order to ascertain if the publishing giant had been poisoned. Maxwell's family said that they didn't wish to speculate about the tests and that they were waiting for the results like anyone else. They added that they had not called for a private investigation. Newspapers were advised that the tests were being carried out for insurance companies, who held a £20 million policy on Maxwell; the policy was payable to his companies and not his family. But, judge Isobel Oliva, who led the investigation into his death, said: "I do not discount anything, absolutely anything." It was certain that he had died from cardiovascular attack, but the causes of the attack were unknown.

At the end of the month, bankers to his companies set up a steering committee to solve the debt problems following his sudden death. His sons Ian, 35, and Kevin, 32, presented 30 top banks with proposals to meet the debts at a meeting in London on 25th November 1991, just three weeks after Maxwell's death. The Maxwell family had already appointed top City bankers Rothschilds as their financial advisers, who were to act jointly with Bankers Trust who already acted for them. Meanwhile, no trace of poison was found in Robert Maxwell's body.

But, by the following month, Ian Maxwell was forced to resign as his father's business deals were probed. He resigned on 3rd December as a massive investigation was launched into millions of pounds that had gone missing from the firm's pension fund, and millions that had gone missing from the Mirror Group itself. The total at the time was estimated at £200 million; most was thought to have disappeared in September and October 1991. Directors of Mirror Group Newspapers (MGN) had discovered "irregular transactions" carried out between the Mirror pension fund and private companies controlled by the late Robert Maxwell. The precise amounts were unclear, but a significant part of the pension fund assets were loaned or transferred to private companies "apparently without due authority". The board then set about fully investigating all the transactions as a matter of urgency and gave assurance that it would: "Do its best to maintain benefits to pension fund members". Ian and Kevin Maxwell both quit the board because of increasing conflicts of interest, while another director, Michael Stoney – who had major management involvement in Maxwell's private companies – also resigned. Ernest Burrington, deputy chairman and joint managing director, was appointed in Ian Maxwell's place following the resignations, while two non-executive directors, Sir Robert Clark and Alan Clements, were appointed joint deputy chairmen. The Maxwell family continued to hold 51 per cent of MGN shares.

By 5th December 1991, a staggering £526 million was known to have vanished from Robert Maxwell's company coffers in the weeks before the tycoon died. And there was no trace of the money, which included £436 million from pension funds. Detectives from the Serious Fraud Office then moved in to probe the mystery of the missing millions amid dark tales of secret midnight meetings called to shift fortunes from place to place. At the time of Maxwell's death, he was coming under increasing pressure to meet massive debts incurred by his private companies. New company chairman Burrington spoke of "the increasingly desperate actions of a desperate man".

Most of the money, it was established, disappeared from the pension funds of three firms – the Mirror Group, Maxwell Communication Corporation and the market research company AGB. A further £100 million had gone missing from Mirror Group accounts – half of it in the last few days before Maxwell fell overboard from his yacht. At this stage, company lawyers had failed to turn up a penny of the money and it was thought that only £100 million of the pensions money would ever be retrieved. Mirror Group staff were told: "It is a nightmare scenario. It's a case of going through drawers and waste-paper baskets looking for scraps of paper." Clandestine late-night meetings had succeeded in moving many millions – and involved very few authorizing signatures.

At the time, Mirror Group pensioners were cheered by the good news that they would continue to receive their money. The fund's trustees confirmed that a substantial sum remained to pay the then existing pensions. It had been decided at an urgent meeting to appoint new directors of Bishopsgate Investment Management (BIM) – the firm managing large amounts of the scheme – to safeguard pension and investments. The government pensions watchdog IMRO confirmed that all but two of the directors of BIM had resigned. It had controlled more than half of the staff pension funds at the Mirror Group. In the years just prior to the fraud, the company had been managing a larger and larger chunk of the pension funds. Businesses chosen for investment were as varied as the size of the sums being shuffled. A 15 per cent stake in Border Television had been bought. The company also moved into retailing and advertising – and even strolled the boards by taking a 15 per cent share of Andrew Lloyd Webber's Really Useful Theatre Company. Some Mirror Group pensioners, meanwhile, were planning to go to the high court over the missing millions; they asked for a receiver to be appointed to the fund to "acquire, find and bring back", the assets of the pension fund.

It then transpired that Maxwell had been dramatically challenged over the missing millions just before his death. His response was to lie. The Mirror Group's finance director, Lawrence Guest, confronted the tycoon and asked about £47 million that had vanished from the newspaper group's coffers. He said at the time that he'd been so worried about it that he was unable to sleep. Maxwell told him: "Don't worry. You are losing sleep and that's not right." He continued: "You will receive everything. Don't worry." In fact, the missing £47 million was just the tip of the iceberg.

It had been Guest's second attempt to confront his boss, but he had been stalled by Maxwell. In confidential notes made after the meeting, Guest wrote: "I am now convinced that MGN resources have been used to support other parts of the group. But I have no proof. I think I have frightened the chairman, but my main concern must be to get the money back." Guest and Maxwell had been due to meet again on 1st November 1991, where Burrington was also poised to ask questions. On the day of the confrontation, Maxwell changed director Stoney's role within MGN and he was suddenly changed from a commercial director to deputy managing director (finance). By the time that Guest's concerns were brought to light in terms of the investigation, solicitors had been appointed to represent the pension trustees in the hunt for the lost cash, and a new company to manage the fund was formed. Meanwhile, shares in Maxwell's Berlitz languages school offshoot were also discovered to have vanished.

With mounting debts, the Maxwell family had to sell off its 51 per cent share to help pay off £1.4 billion. Most of the stake was pledged to banks as collateral for loans to Maxwell family companies. MGN, including the *Mirror*, the *Sunday Mirror*, *The People*, the *Daily Record*, *Sunday Mail* and *Sporting Life* were to be sold as a whole and not divided up. John Talbot, appointed as joint administrator in December 1991, was asked whether or not the politics of a prospective buyer would be taken into account and replied: "We tend to deal on commercial grounds. It is more a matter of money." However, the *Mirror* was determined not to fall into Tory hands. Journalists had just voted unanimously to fight for the *Mirror*'s traditions and policies – including support for the Labour Party. On 6th December 1991, staff of the Mirror Group united in a bid to buy the company's newspapers. The move was announced by *Mirror* editor Richard Stott who, along with colleagues, had brought in top British investment group Electra. Stott said: "It is the staff who have made our newspapers great. They deserve the chance to control their own destiny." News of the buyout was welcomed by staff, readers and politicians.

The editor then wrote a letter to the readership – printed in the newspaper on Saturday 7th December 1991 – thanking them for their support during what must have been one of the most desperate months for the newspaper and its staff. It was a letter that described Maxwell as: "Far from going down as the man who saved this great national institution he will be remembered, I'm afraid, as the man who nearly destroyed it. A thief and a liar." Had he been alive to read the letter, it would undoubtedly have come as a blow to the man who had wanted to be remembered for quite the opposite reason. The letter made a heart-felt thanks to its readership for standing by the newspaper.

Meanwhile, it transpired that Lawrence Guest's office had been bugged.

A voice-activated wire tap was found in his office telephone. The wire led to a tape recorder (which was Maxwell's own) in an office where security chiefs were based. The wires – which were still active when found – snaked from Guest's office on the ninth floor of Mirror Group's headquarters at London's Holborn Circus to the office of Ernest Burrington, where a signal booster had been hidden behind the room's panelling. The wires continued through the Mirror HQ, across to the building next door – also owned by the Maxwell empire – and on to a nearby office at 52 Fetter Lane. This final office was that of John Pole, director of group security for Maxwell Communication Corporation.

John Pole handed over the tapes of the group's executives' conversations. More than £20,000 had been spent on bugging the offices of Guest and bosses of two other Maxwell companies, when the publishing man had grown increasingly paranoid that plotters were out to get him. To start with, Maxwell had been given unedited tapes but, after he played them at top volume continuously, it was feared that those being bugged would hear themselves. So, he was then presented with edited versions. Pole had let slip to former bodyguard Les Williams that he was "looking after" Guest. Williams then told the finance director of his suspicions over bugging and the wire tap was soon discovered. Meanwhile, the spouse pension being paid to Betty Maxwell was stopped by the Mirror Group while pension fund officials studied a rule which said that relatives of a fund member are not entitled to payments if the member had committed a criminal, fraudulent or negligent act.

Maxwell had known that he was on the verge of being exposed for illegal share trading when he fell off his yacht. A note found on the *Lady Ghislaine* showed that US bankers were threatening to act over secret multi-million pound loans the tycoon had failed to repay. The loans had bcen securcd against shares that he had not been entitled to trade in. The Communications Corporation had disclosed that part of its stake in the Berlitz language school had gone missing, delaying its sale to a Japanese company. The message also appeared to show that the missing shares were being seized by bankers Lehman Brothers.

Meanwhile, financial whizz-kid Larry Trachtenberg – who transferred blue chip shares to Maxwell's personal safe – had gone into hiding. He had quit Maxwell's HQ in early December and hadn't been seen at his home in London. Trachtenberg had served on the boards of BIM and London and Bishopsgate International Investment Management (LBIIM). (BIM was handed stewardship of money from pension funds before it was funnelled to LBIIM.) On 9th December 1991, Fraud Squad police raided a strongroom at the hub of Maxwell's empire and found that "the cupboard was bare". The swoop on the walk-in safe in the office of Maxwell's finance director was to look for the missing millions, but they found only empty shelves. At the same time, Kevin Maxwell's £450 million assets were frozen by the high court. Both Ian and Kevin Maxwell were ordered to surrender their passports and both were given seven days in which to reveal anything they might have known about the missing £426 million from pension funds.

Appearing at the high court, Kevin Maxwell had to report on how he was co-operating with attempts to track down the cash plundered by his cheating father. He told a judge that he would exercise his right to remain silent in case he faced charges. Meanwhile, it emerged that Maxwell family companies borrowed money against shares held by the Mirror Group pension fund two days after Maxwell's death. The shares – in the Israeli medicines firm Teva – were offered to NatWest Bank as security for a £15 million loan. NatWest said that it took the shares in good faith and only sealed the deal after having received written representation from the family companies that they owned the shares. Writs were then served against Ian and Kevin and their father's estate, claiming back money belonging to Mirror Group Newspapers. A further 294 writs were also issued against Maxwell companies around the world.

Both sons were eventually given back their passports – Ian so he could join his American-born wife in the States for a break after it was announced he was suffering from acute stress syndrome, and Kevin so that he could attend crucial meetings in New York. Both promised not to abscond. The accountants warned that the communication's debts could turn out to be more than the £1.6 billion estimated at that stage, and the skipper of Maxwell's yacht revealed how the tycoon's daughter had shredded a large number of documents on-board the vessel in the hours following her father's death.

By the end of December 1991 evidence had come to light that Robert Maxwell and two of his sons removed £170 million from Mirror Group Newspapers. Charles Falconer, QC, told the high court that £120 million was taken out on the authority of the late publisher. A further £39 million was removed in the name of Ian and £11 million on the authority of Kevin. Kevin's counsel, Michael Briggs, said that a charge of conspiracy to defraud was theoretically on the cards. At the beginning of 1992, it transpired that the younger Maxwell had written a letter assuring directors of Maxwell Communication Corporation (MCC) that money moved out of the company had not been used for illegal purposes, which he co-signed with his father. In January 1992, it was announced that most of the assets plundered from the Mirror Group pension fund had been held by banks as security for money lent to Robert Maxwell.

The tycoon robbed the pension funds by "borrowing" its shares under a process called "stock lending". Then he offered them to banks as security for loans; much of the money taken was then used to buy £400 million worth of MCC shares. He re-registered the shares in his own, or a family company name; about half the deals were done illegally. The aim was to prop up the MCC share price, because Maxwell had already used most of his MCC shares as security for bank loans to family companies. The rest of the missing money was used mainly to meet losses and payments on family businesses and borrowings. The Maxwell family empire debts – at that time – were estimated at

£1.4 billion and all its assets were up for sale. It took auditors just two days to discover that £428 million was missing from the pension funds once they were given access to the books.

Most of the cash, MPs were told in the Commons in February 1992, were shares sold without the funds being repaid. Evidence showed that £118 million was not recovered from sales of shares in an Israeli firm, £57 million of MCC shares were disposed of by Maxwell, £193 million stocks were lent to unknown parties, and £60 million vanished in shares whose ownership remained unclear.

The companies' books due to be examined in March 1991 had been rescheduled for November that same year instead. That month the board also announced that the old pension scheme was to be wound up and a new one created, which was welcomed by trustees. By March 1992, both Maxwell brothers were set to face the full wrath of Parliament if they did not end their silence over the missing money. They even faced jail if they refused to co-operate with an all-party select committee of MPs.

By May 1992, all eyes were on bungling ministers and trade officials who had allowed Maxwell to plunder his workers' pension funds, while it was also claimed that unless there was urgent government action, more than 6,000 pensioners faced destitution by September. More than £450 million was still missing and the government was blasted by Ken Trench, chairman of the Maxwell Pensioners' Action Group, for ignoring the plight of pensioners robbed of their money. Peter Lilley, the social security secretary, was handed evidence that month that there had been a failure by ministers to prevent the fraud. It was also claimed that Maxwell had "hoodwinked" the Department of Trade.

In June 1992, NatWest refused to give back pension money amounting to £31 million plundered by Maxwell despite a plea by Colin Cornwall, chairman of the Mirror Group scheme, that thousands of people were facing poverty.

Also that month, pensioners fleeced by the tycoon demanded a judicial inquiry into the scandal following claims that the government knew about the suspicious business dealings before Maxwell plundered £450 million. Government GCHQ eavesdroppers are said to have bugged Maxwell's business empire two years before he died, with reports going to the prime minister's office, cabinet ministers and the Bank of England. The government, led by John Major, was said to have let Maxwell have two investment licences after it was warned about him by GCHQ and that these licences were then used to plunder the pensions. The Bank of England, however, denied any intelligence reports and said that it had no access to sensitive information. But, the *Financial Times*, which reported the claims, said its story was confirmed by another source.

Both Ian and Kevin Maxwell were brought up on charges that included stealing portfolios of securities. The two were accused of Britain's biggest financial fraud after being arrested, together with Trachtenberg, in dawn swoops. Their bail was raised by friends and both vowed to challenge the charges against them. But, at the end of June they were to face more charges. Meanwhile, NatWest agreed to return £27 million of the pension assets that it had known for months were stolen. The move was destined to put pressure on Credit Suisse,

Banque Nationale de Paris and Lehman Brothers to hand back funds totaling £120 million, which they too knew were stolen. And, IMRO, finally admitted that its handling of Maxwell and the Mirror Group pension was lax. It transpired in the middle of 1992 that Maxwell's death had most likely been suicide.

In February 1995, the pensions of 32,000 victims of the fraud were made safe when a major settlement was reached with big City investment firms. In June that same year, both Maxwell sons, Trachtenberg and former director and financial aide to Maxwell, Robert Bunn, all stood charged with conspiring together between 5th November and 21st November 1991 to defraud the trustees and beneficiaries of pension schemes in the Common Investment Fund by dishonestly putting at risk 25,196,228 shares in Teva Pharmaceutical Industries by suing them for the purposes of the Robert Maxwell Group. After a tense eight-month trial, Ian and Kevin Maxwell left the Old Bailey as free men, cleared of fraud. Headlines in the *Mirror* read: "GUILTY of being born to a bullying cheat called Maxwell". Another article read: "Maxwell was a monster, a crook, a grand deceiver and a bully – even to his own family". The jury decided that Maxwell, and Maxwell alone, was responsible for plundering more than £500 million from the Mirror Group and its pension funds. It was increasingly unlikely that anyone would pay the price for his crimes, which were "the most despicable non-violent offences of the century". The pension fund was replenished, bringing security to pensioners and the *Mirror* was restored and became stronger than ever. The *Mirror* said: "No legacy remains of Maxwell's corruption and abuse of this newspaper. We have risen above his evil."

Nick Leeson

(1995)

The hunt was under way on 26th February 1995 for the British whizz-kid who triggered the collapse of the Queen's merchant bank. Investigators wanted to question 28-year-old Nick Leeson, a Singapore-based trader who lost Barings up to £450 million in disastrous stock-market gambling. Barings was tiny compared to the "Big Four" – Barclays, NatWest, Lloyds and Midland – which together formed one of the safest banking systems in the world. Yet Leeson's complex deals had plunged blue-blooded Barings, Britain's oldest merchant bank, into crisis. As Bank of England chiefs worked on a rescue package, a Barings spokeswoman said: "There is a very high suspicion of fraud." But, ordinary bank customers were told they had no reason to worry.

Leeson, meanwhile, had left substantial debts in Britain. It was discovered that he owed more than £3,000 on county court judgments, while Barings confirmed that they had made no financial checks on him prior to giving him a plum job. Leeson, who earned around £200,000 a year including commissions, failed to turn up to work in the week prior to the bank's collapse and was thought to have fled to Singapore. He'd joined the bank three years previously and led a life as a top financial trader – a world apart from his early years on a council estate in Watford, Hertfordshire.

Eddie George, the then governor of the Bank of England, headed a rescue operation while stock markets around the world braced themselves for a massive shock reaction to the Barings crash. Worried inspectors were already investigating Leeson's transactions before the huge losses were revealed. Stunned Barings director Sir William Ryrie wasn't able to shed any further light on the problems, but the bank was one of the firms that looked after the Queen's £158 million fortune. It played a leading role in managing Prince Charles's Duchy of Cornwall estates and Barings' director Lord Ashburton had helped Prince Charles turn in a £4 million profit from the £30 million holding in 1994. The queen, who was said to be "shocked", was being kept informed, although her money was said to be safe. The Bank of England desperately tried to find a buyer for Barings, but if one wasn't found quickly then the Bank of England would have to step in by using taxpayers' money to guarantee debts to bail out the crashed bank. Up to 4,000 jobs at the bank were on the line (2,000 of them in Bishopsgate, London). It was thought that Leeson had gambled extremely large sums through derivatives – risky financial instruments – which could lead to massive losses.

Barings could trace its roots back to 1762 when, as the oldest merchant bank in London, it had been a trading house dealing in wool, timber, copper and diamonds. It branched out and by 1818 was regarded as one of the greatest powers in Europe. The bank helped fund the Napoleonic wars for Britain and was a major player in international finance in the 19th century. But, in 1890, it came badly unstuck over investments in Argentina and had to be rescued by the Bank of England. The Baring family was virtually bankrupt but, by the 1920s, the bank was back on top. During the 1980s it started specializing in the Japanese markets. Its efforts there were a spectacular success and the executive in charge was made Britain's highest-paid director in 1989, with £3 million earnings. The Baring family was still in control at the time of the collapse, with the then current chairman, Peter Baring, having been in his post since the end of the 1980s. At the time of the bank's crash, it had been expected to make profits of £120 million in 1995.

Meanwhile, runaway dealer Leeson was believed to be a mega-fraudster who had deliberately sabotaged the bank with the help of a mystery accomplice. And, it was believed that the two were cashing in on the bank's £800 million losses (announced in February 1995). As a worldwide hunt continued for Leeson, Chairman Peter Baring outlined how the alleged sting could have been carried out. It transpired that Leeson had likely been hiding financial transactions that had secretly been set up as loss-making deals for Barings in Singapore, which it was reckoned had gone undetected since 1994. Leeson could then have profited from the resulting falling market as the bank inevitably failed. It was suspected that the trader was also involved in financial frauds involving the Asian money markets.

The shock waves from the disastrous dealing sent money markets plummeting all over the world. About £2.5 billion was wiped off shares in London, while investigators discovered that Leeson's derivatives trading – with gambles on share-price movements – potentially had up to £17 billion to play with. The Tokyo market plunged, and tourists leaving Britain for holidays abroad saw their spending power slump in the wake of the crisis. The pound hit an all-time low against the German mark and slumped against most other European currencies.

Barings believed that Leeson had teamed up with accomplices to siphon off money into secret unauthorized bank accounts. Auditors had failed to uncover the fraud prior to the crisis because the bulk of it happened in the few weeks leading up to the crash. Some believed that Leeson could have been "receiving inducements". However, he could equally have simply been gambling and then having to double and re-double to try to cover and recoup his losses.

Porsche-driving Nick Leeson dealt in stock-market billions – even though he failed A-level maths. He'd been described by colleagues as a "brilliant but abrasive loner, an arrogant show-off who liked to make a big impression". However, another colleague described him as: "a rather sad character striving to be popular, but he just didn't seem to have the necessary qualifications". He had vowed to make a million while still in his humble surroundings in Watford and he quickly clawed his way from a 1960s council house to a life of luxury in Singapore. It was thought that after fleeing Singapore, Leeson and his 26-year-old wife, Lisa, were hiding in Thailand. In the 12 months before the crash, Leeson was known to have pocketed £3 million from his dealings. He was eventually found at a posh hotel in Kuala Lumpur. He checked into the Regent Hotel in Malaysia after entering the country on a forged passport. It was believed that he was short of funds and there was a warrant out for his arrest. However, he'd been paid a £400,000 bonus in 1994 and some Singapore traders put his bonus as high as £1 million. There were signs of a hurried departure from his fifth-floor apartment in Singapore.

The maverick dealer had already boasted to colleagues that he'd made enough money to retire the following year. After checking into the Regent Hotel, he disappeared the following day. It was thought he'd gone to Malaysia rather than less risky escape routes in order to pick up cash banked in the city of Kuala Lumpur. Then, in March 1995, it seemed as if the net was closing in on the rogue trader amid reports that Thai police had discovered his hiding place. Senior officials in Bangkok refused to comment, but the hunt was concentrating on the towns of Krabi and Trang in the south of the country. Leeson's photograph had been widely circulated, which would have made it harder for him to move around. And, despite there being no extradition treaty between Singapore and Thailand, Thai officials vowed to send him back. However, the couple were eventually detained at Frankfurt Airport in March as they stepped off a flight from Brunei. Leeson claimed to be on his way back to London to clear his name.

He was detained in a German police cell pending formal extradition proceedings from Singapore authorities. Leeson had told a friend that he'd escaped from Singapore as he was being set up as a scapegoat for the Barings bank crash. And he said that in his work he had acted with the "authority of people in head office in London". When it all went wrong, he claimed, he realized that he was going to have to take the sole blame. At this point, he faced up to four months in a German jail while the fight continued to send him back to Singapore.

But, as Leeson faced court in Frankfurt, a secret Fraud Squad inquiry into Barings had found evidence of swindling in London that could possibly lead to a worldwide conspiracy. London City police agreed that Leeson could be an important witness and even suggested that he could be the key to exposing top bosses. Leeson, for his part, shouted at the

German judge who ordered him back behind bars to await extradition proceedings to Singapore. Three officials from Singapore delivered preliminary documents to German authorities, outlining their reasons, but Leeson's lawyer argued that Singapore's request was not appropriate; the legal system was not the same as the UK's and human rights were not sufficient. The British legal system was preferable. Meanwhile, the lawyer also offered a warning to Barings bank stating that his client had information that could damage other people at the bank.

Bosses at Barings suspected up to eight months before the bank's collapse that Leeson was a danger and they were warned in an internal report two months later that it was possible to override their systems for checking deals. City insiders said at the time that the revelations seemed to support Leeson's claim that he was being made a scapegoat. The findings of the 24-page report should have set alarm bells ringing. Then Leeson agreed to tell all and blow the whistle on bosses at Barings bank by talking to Britain's Serious Fraud Squad. His lawyer argued that anyone believing that a rogue trader could bring the bank down on his own was being "unrealistic". Leeson's two lawyers, Stephen Pollard and Eberhard Kempf, agreed that they would go to extraordinary lengths to get him returned to Britain, including filing charges against him in the UK. But, on 24th March 1995, it seemed set that he would face trial in Singapore. It was a bitter blow to the 28-year-old; a UK inquiry involving the Bank of England and the Serious Fraud Squad would take months to complete. Just two months' later, Barings got rid of 21 top bosses for failing to control the rogue dealer.

In return for "going quietly", the 21 affected staff were given a payoff, including Peter Norris, the chief executive, and William Daniel, the Japanese branch manager. James Bax, Leeson's boss in Singapore, was also asked to leave. Peter Baring and his deputy Andrew Tuckey had already quit the bank. However, no blame was attached to the 21 employees. In a letter to then Prime Minister John Major, Leeson admitted that he caused the bank to collapse and that he would plead guilty. He promised to accept the charges against him if he could go to a British jail. He was desperate to avoid Changi Prison in Singapore.

In September 1995, a TV programme was aired in which Leeson spoke for two hours to Sir David Frost for a BBC one-off, *The Man Who Broke the Bank*. He told how he recklessly gambled with Barings' money on the lucrative but risky futures market in Singapore; there were days when he lost £30 million but other days where he made £50 million. In 1992, he began hiding his losses in a secret account but had sleepless nights throughout 1993 and 1994 as debts rocketed. When the debts reached £350 million, alarm bells began to ring in London and the game was up. Leeson said he never expected the bank to collapse and insisted that he didn't steal any money. Instead he said: "I was trying to correct a situation."

In October 1995, three top executives at Barings were accused of covering up the disastrous dealings of Leeson. The damning report blamed Peter Norris, James Bax and Anthony Hawes, the group treasurer, of inefficiency, incompetence and a cover-up. Leeson eventually faced a Singapore court in December 1995 and admitted to two counts of fraud. Prosecutors did not believe that he acted alone. Nine other charges were dropped after he agreed to co-operate with investigators and to pay £70,000 in prosecution costs. It was believed he would serve a two- or three-year jail term which, with time off for good behaviour, could have seen him return home in months (he'd already been held for nine months by this time). However, he would have to face the notorious Changi Prison where armed guards were known to be ready to shoot if necessary – and he was actually sentenced to six and a half years. The following year it was discovered that there were six accounts in Germany that required Leeson's signature, and investigators began to suspect that far from not making any money from the bank's collapse, the former trader probably did have a "pot of gold" out there somewhere.

In 1998, Leeson was diagnosed with cancer and his former wife, Lisa, postponed her wedding to new love Keith Horlock. She felt it was inappropriate to marry when her ex-husband was so ill. Until the publication of Leeson's book, Lisa had stood by her former husband, but the extent of his deception and the double life he'd led shook her to the core. Leeson was initially given a 40 per cent chance of survival by experts and there were moves to bring the fraudster back to Britain. Later that same year, it was revealed that Leeson's father was also suffering from cancer and was too ill to visit his son in Singapore. A tumour removed from Nick Leeson's colon showed that the cancer had not spread and his prognosis was a little better than had been feared. He was released from his Singapore jail in July 1999; he had served four years and four months for bringing down Barings.

In 2005 Leeson went on to become commercial director of Galway United in Ireland.

Enron

– The NatWest Three

At the end of November 2001, the proposed £9.6 billion takeover of PowerGen looked set to founder if the business of one of its American rivals continued to deteriorate. The company's City shareholders were panicking that German utility group Eon would try to back off from its proposal to buy its rival. Around half of the electricity generator was owned by arbitrage fund managers who were nervous about some of PowerGen's American business. PowerGen, set to be bought by Eon for a hefty 765p a share in cash, bought and sold electricity from troubled US rival Enron. Just one day before, Enron's stock plunged 70 per cent after its own merger partner, Dynegy, pulled out of a US$9 billion merger.

Up to this point, PowerGen had refused to "come clean" about the precise extent of its exposure to Enron. It had tried to pacify shareholders by claiming that its exposure was not "material" when it unveiled nine-month figures at the start of that same month. But, on 28th November 2001, Wall Street credit-rating agencies said they thought that Enron's financial health was deteriorating, and they branded the company's bonds as "junk". Enron shares collapsed from $90 in August 2000 to just over $1 at the end of November. One analyst said: "The Germans still need to get the go-ahead from some very prickly regulators before the deal to buy PowerGen can go ahead. It is by no means a done deal." The City was not convinced PowerGen would actually be bought; while Eon offered a value of 765p per share, the stock were only fetching 741p (8p of which was an imminent dividend payment). The European Competition Commission had given the "green light" for the deal, but the United States' Securities and Exchange Commission still needed to clear it early in 2002. A PowerGen spokesman said: "We do have an exposure to Enron, but we're not saying what it is. It is managed within the group's overall controlled risk strategy. The board signs it off."

However, on 30th November, banks were rocked by the biggest corporate collapse in history. Abbey National faced losses of up to £95 million and its shares plunged by 6 per cent as US energy giant Enron teetered on the brink of bankruptcy. Other banks were also expected to report losses, and PricewaterhouseCoopers (PwC) were appointed as administrators to Enron's European holding company. The firm had already axed more than 1,000 jobs in the UK due to the crisis. Tony Lomas, a partner of PwC said there were only limited funds available, so releasing a large number of people was inevitable. The cuts were believed to be at Enron's energy trading HQ in London, with just 250 staff in the capital being kept on. But Enron's other UK divisions, including Wessex Water and power stations in Teesside, avoided administration and were believed to have remained unaffected at that time. Enron, based in Houston, Texas, had debts of £10 billion and had been pushed to the brink by a shock £857 million charge that related to one of its companies. The company's fate was sealed when the multi-billion-dollar merger talks with rival Dynegy fell through. National Australia Bank – which owned Yorkshire Bank and Clydesdale Bank in the UK – also revealed the Enron effect by saying that it had secured and unsecured links to the company of around £141 million. After the company's collapse, British banks faced losses of up to £670 million.

The American company's UK subsidiaries were thought to owe huge amounts to banks, including Barclays, Royal Bank of Scotland (RBS) and Abbey National. Abbey had already announced that it had lent the company £115 million and expected to lose £95 million. However, Barclays and RBS refused to comment on reports that they were owed cash by Enron, but their total exposure was estimated to be around £140 million for RBS and between £50 million and £300 million for Barclays. Enron had run into difficulties when it spent billions on telecoms companies that were outside its main line of business – generating and supplying energy, and trading gas and electricity.

The crisis facing Enron – or Enrongate, as it became known in the press – deepened at the beginning of 2002 when it emerged that Ken Lay, boss of Enron, had been warned that the company would "implode" two months before it actually went bust. Lay had been warned of disaster by a senior executive, Vice President Sherron Watkins, who wrote: "I am incredibly nervous that we will implode in a wave of accounting scandals." She added that a "veil of secrecy" surrounded deals, keeping huge debts off the company's books. The company had, by this time, filed the largest bankruptcy case in US history and a criminal investigation had been launched by the Justice Department. Meanwhile, trading in the company's shares was suspended as auditors Arthur Andersen fired the man in charge of the Enron account.

By the end of January 2002, Downing Street was under pressure over the £10 billion worth of government contracts with a firm at the heart of the Enron disaster. Arthur Andersen, the consultancy and accountancy giant being probed over the collapse, was involved with at least 37 taxpayer-funded contracts, including projects in hospitals, schools and the London Tube. Further, the government found itself under fire over financial and political links with the failed energy company and its auditors. Andersen was facing corporate meltdown after shock revelations about the mass shredding of sensitive documents linked to Enron's £55 billion crash – which was the world's largest bankruptcy. And, there were fears over a number of Andersen's unfinished government contracts if Enron was found guilty by US investigators.

Tony Blair, the then prime minister, told Labour's National Executive Committee meeting that there had been no wrongdoing. Meanwhile, Tory and Liberal Democrat MPs demanded an inquiry into allegations that the government lifted a ban on the building of gas-fired power stations to benefit Enron. Downing Street rejected claims that Enron had influenced energy policy with a £38,000 donation to Labour. The government also denied allegations of sleaze in what had been dubbed "the cash-for-access storm". There were strong calls for the government to suspend or review Andersen's private finance initiative (PFI) contracts until the Enron investigation was complete.

Meanwhile, reporters had a field day with the story, with accusations that Enron bought access to Blair and his ministers, and influenced a critical shift in government energy policy away from coal to gas. Suspicions pointed to the fact that Blair and his sidekick, Peter Mandelson, welcomed the wealthy businessmen who beat a path to their door. They wrongly assumed that big business wanted to invest in the New Labour project. When Formula One king Bernie Ecclestone gave the party £1 million, a government ban on tobacco advertising – a ban that was undesirable to the Formula One industry due to the amount of revenue they gained from it – was averted. Journalists argued that this was Ecclestone "Mark 2". Enron had reversed Labour's policy of no more gas-fired power stations, which were killing the coal industry in which thousands of miners lost their jobs. And Blair had to apologize over Ecclestone and hand back the money he'd donated to the party. The Enron scandal couldn't have come at a worse time for the government. It had debts of £10 million and no way of repaying the money.

Small firms Houston Natural Gas and InterNorth merged in Houston to form Enron in 1986. By 2000, it was the seventh-largest US firm with a staff of 20,000 in 30 countries. In 1999, the firm set up an internet-based system of trading in future prices of energy. A year later, the £1.4 billion firm was worth £50 billion, but Enron had been hiding its debts from investors. At the time of the collapse, the firm owed £55 billion, which was known to top executives who still cashed in on stock. The first warning signs came in May 2001 when Vice President Clifford Baxter quit, but it took the whistle-blowing of Sherron Watkins to bring the scandal to light.

Enron, as one of the biggest contributors to President Bush's campaign – along with 75 per cent of senators and congressmen having accepted donations – wasn't just reflecting badly on UK politics. There were even claims that the White House changed an energy proposal to help Enron in India; disgraced chairman Ken Lay was said to have close links to President Bush. The company first became involved in the UK when it bought Wessex Water for £1.5 billion in 1998. The Enron donations gave the company access to UK ministers, although all impropriety was denied. Those who had lost were the Florida state pension fund – to the tune of £230 million – and Enron employees who lost their life savings.

The first criminal charges came in March 2002 when Arthur Andersen faced the courts over the collapse. The Justice Department in the US charged Andersen with obstructing justice by shredding "tons of paper" in offices across the world, including London. The indictment claimed that staff working on the cover-up used a shredder "virtually consistently" and were ordered to do overtime to destroy papers in "dozens of trunks". Deputy Attorney General Larry Thompson said that staff engaged in "the wholesale destruction" of materials, which extended far beyond the firm's headquarters in Texas. He continued: "It shouldn't be a surprise to anyone that serious charges have serious consequences." The indictment was made public after the firm failed to meet a deadline to agree to plead guilty. It said that Andersen "did knowingly, intentionally and corruptly persuade employees to alter, destroy, mutilate and conceal documents". The watchdog Securities and Exchange Commission had announced it was conducting an inquiry into Enron just before the shredding began. Andersen – headed by Chief Executive Joseph Berardino – angrily complained that the charges would bring down the accounting giant. The maximum penalty was five years' probation and a £300,000 fine. Meanwhile, President Bush was trying to distance himself from the scandal. The ex-boss of Enron was paid more than £70 million before the firm actually went bust. Lay had pocketed a cool £7 million pension and a £60 million loan – most of which he repaid using shares awarded by Enron. In addition, other top executives were paid £220 million before the bankruptcy; the sums were detailed in papers filed at New York's bankruptcy court in June 2002. A lawyer for Enron employees who lost pensions in the collapse said: "It's evident people at the top knew they better get, while the going was good."

In January 2004, husband and wife team Andrew and Lea Fastow swapped their luxury home for jail because of their role in the scandal. Andrew had been chief finance officer at the former energy giant and faced a 10-year jail sentence after he admitted "cooking the books" at Enron. He also forfeited around £16 million and an unfinished Houston mansion. His wife, who had been assistant treasurer at the company, faced five months behind bars after admitting one count of filling a false tax return. Fastow, who co-operated with investigators and thus escaped what could have amounted to a life sentence, was the biggest coup for the authorities at the time. Officials hinted that his arrest and subsequent conviction would help in the case against Enron kingpins, including Lay and Jeff Skilling, a former chief executive. Skilling claimed that he had been made the scapegoat when, in February 2004, he was charged with 36 counts of fraud, insider trading and lying about the firm's finances. He was, at this time, the most senior executive to be indicted. However, he denied all charges and claimed that he believed the company to have been in good health.

But, in June 2006 more shocking news came to light when three NatWest bankers began fighting extradition to America over "skimming" £11 million in what was a "quintessential inside job". Planned by Gary Mulgrew, Giles Darby and David Bermingham, the three were alleged to have "skimmed for themselves" £1.3 million each in a deal that siphoned £4.1 million via a bank in the Cayman Islands. They were accused of using their positions at the bank's investment arm to concoct the scam with bosses at Enron. All three denied the allegations and were not charged with any offences in the UK, but on 21st June, the US Government asked a London court to extradite the three to face trial in Texas. If found guilty of "wire fraud" they were facing jail for five years.

Acting for US prosecutors, John Hardy told Bow Street Magistrates Court in London that the men hatched a plan with Enron bosses Andrew Fastow and Michael Kopper; the two Americans had both pleaded guilty to fraud charges. It was alleged that the British trio persuaded NatWest to sell their stake in an Enron-linked investment company for just $1 million when they knew it was worth up to $20 million. Reading a statement from an FBI agent, Hardy told the court: "This was the quintessential inside job because NatWest did not know about the robbery until the collapse of Enron." He explained that complex transactions through an offshore bank allowed the three men to "pocket the difference themselves".

Mulgrew was furious that the trio were not given the chance to defend themselves in the UK. The 42-year-old Scotsman claimed that they would not get a fair trial in the US. The three retained the services of hard-hitting barrister Alun Jones to argue that under British law the US had no right to haul them across the Atlantic. But, in September 2004, it was suspected that the British bankers were being used as bait by US prosecutors. Jones told Bow Street Magistrates Court that the three men were being targeted to implicate senior Enron figures. However, the three men vowed to fight on after they lost their court battle over the extradition to the US on 21st February 2006. The high court said that Mulgrew, Darby and Bermingham should be tried in Texas; the three were expected to appeal to the Lords. The case was seen as the first big test of the 2003 Extradition Act, which the government had said was necessary in order to fight terrorism. Despite the fact that the men's lawyers claimed that, as UK citizens accused of defrauding a UK bank, they should be prosecuted in Britain, Lord Justice Laws and Justice Ouseley argued that it would be "unduly simplistic to treat the case as a domestic affair".

In May 2006, both Lay and Skilling were found guilty of fraud and conspiracy. It had taken a four-year probe into Enron's collapse to bring the two men to justice. Skilling, 52, was found guilty of 19 of the 28 charges, while Lay, 64, was found guilty of all six charges brought against him. The two were also accused of lying to investors about the company's financial problems and, in a separate case, Lay was found guilty of four charges of bank fraud totalling £40 million. But, just one month later, on 5th July 2006, Lay dropped dead from a massive heart attack. The disgraced boss – who was born into poverty but once boasted a £100 million fortune – had been expected to face decades behind bars for his part in the Enron scandal. Sentencing had yet to take place. Lay had steadfastly denied the charges and proclaimed himself innocent even after his convictions. Meanwhile, Tony Blair hinted in the Commons that the NatWest Three may not go to jail pending their trials. However, he refused to block their extradition to Texas. On 13th July 2006, the three were extradited.

The men, who claimed they had "been screwed", said tearful farewells to their families before boarding a flight to Houston to face trial for the alleged £11 million fraud. Their lawyer, Mark Spragg, claimed that they faced an unfair trial in the US. He also said that they would have to put their assets on the line to get bail and, if refused, they could spend months in detention. The three men had to surrender to Croydon police station before being driven to Gatwick Airport. It was claimed that, after persuading NatWest to sell part of a company owned by Enron for less than it was worth, the men then left the bank and bought a stake in the company, which they then sold for a much higher price. Jeff Skilling was jailed for 24 years.

On 22nd February 2008, the three former NatWest bankers were jailed for three years each and ordered to repay £3.5 million to the NatWest owners, RBS. They had pleaded guilty to the charges in November 2007. Judge Ewing Welein Jr in Texas said: "In order to regain respect you will have to pay back every pound."